365
HOPEFUL
DEVOTIONS
—— *for* ——
CATHOLICS

DAILY MOMEN

CW01090743

Creative Communications for the Parish
1564 Fencorp Drive
Fenton, MO 63026
www.creativecommunications.com

365 Hopeful Devotions for Catholics: Daily Moments with God
was compiled by Pat Gohn, Ciera Clivio, Alison Foley, Kasey Nugent and
Karen Tucker for Creative Communications for the Parish,
1564 Fencorp Drive, Fenton, MO 63026. 800-325-9414.

www.livingfaith.com
www.creativecommunications.com

ISBN: 978-1-68279-395-4

Cover photo: Shutterstock.com
Cover design: Jeff McCall

Printed in the U.S.A.

Other books by *Living Faith* include:

365 Devotions for Catholics: Daily Moments with God

365 Devotions for Catholic Women: Daily Moments with God

Living Faith: Prayers for Catholics

Reading God's Word

Living Faith Kids Sticker Booklets

Praying the Mass

Learning About the Sacraments

Praying the Rosary

Learning All About Mary

Meet Pope Francis

Learning About the Ten Commandments

Praying the Stations of the Cross

What I See in Church

Living the Beatitudes

What We Do in Advent

What We Do in Lent

Learning About the Works of Mercy

Learning About the Bible

Heroes of the Old Testament

Heroes of the New Testament

Miracles of Jesus

Receive the Lord

God's Gift of Forgiveness

TABLE OF CONTENTS

INTRODUCTION

> **...HOPE does not disappoint, because the love of God has been poured out into our hearts through the holy Spirit that has been given to us.** Romans 5:5

Hope is a God thing. It is not wishful thinking or a positive attitude or happy talk. It is of an order of magnitude much greater than the limits of our imagination or anything that our mortal world might try to describe. For it is grounded in something otherworldly: It is an infused virtue, rooted in the promise of heaven and given to us personally by God in Baptism.

Hope lives in the mercy received from the Cross of Christ and the glory of the Risen Lord fresh from the tomb. It is alive in the Communion Rite at every Mass, both in the coming of Jesus in the Blessed Sacrament and in our prayers for his coming again as "we await the blessed hope and the coming of our Savior, Jesus Christ." The *Catechism of the Catholic Church*, paragraph 2090, keeps it pithy: "Hope is the confident expectation of divine blessing and the beatific vision of God."

Hope anticipates blessings we expect to come. Authentic hope is a hallmark of Christian living. While it is associated with our future, hope animates the *now* of our lives—enriching this present moment with an eternal perspective. For those who follow Jesus, the promise of life eternal—the hope of heaven—is real. Such hope is not based on what we might possibly do; it is based on what God does. God not only opened a path to heaven for us but offers us the graces we need to attain it.

Yet there are times when our sense of hope may wane. We may be struggling and searching for a beacon of hope. It is then and there we must turn to Jesus. He is our true hope, the restorer and healer of our souls. And so, we must pray, asking Jesus for the hope we need. Pope Francis has taught: "Prayer is the first strength of hope. You pray and hope grows, it moves forward. ...Prayer opens the door to hope. ...Men and women who pray know that hope is stronger than discouragement" (General Audience, May 20, 2020).

Indeed, hope is a God thing. But it is also a God-given thing— offered generously by the One who knows us best.

My thanks and gratitude to the many writers who penned these meditations and our team at *Living Faith* who curated them. May this book spark your own conversations with the God of Hope who loves you and is always faithful.

May the God of hope fill you with all joy and peace in believing, so that you may abound in hope by the power of the holy Spirit (Romans 15:13).

Pat Gohn
Editor, *Living Faith: Daily Catholic Devotions*

A Prayer of Hope

Hope, O my soul, hope. You know neither the day nor the hour. Watch carefully, for everything passes quickly, even though your impatience makes doubtful what is certain, and turns a very short time into a long one. Dream that the more you struggle, the more you prove the love that you bear your God, and the more you will rejoice one day with your Beloved, in a happiness and rapture that can never end.

St. Teresa of Avila

Promise of Hope

May the eyes of [your] hearts be enlightened, that you may know what is the hope that belongs to his call... Ephesians 1:18

Hope can be a fragile, elusive emotion. Hardly a day goes by when we don't hope for something—good health, world peace...or just making the next green light. But who among us hasn't seen our hopes just as easily dashed, gone in an instant? The trigger could be the sudden loss of a job or the untimely death of a loved one. Without hope, we enter a void, a disturbing place where every deeply held belief can be called into question, including and especially our faith. Hope is the embodiment of the Christian message. It won't disappear. It is always there, always beckoning when all seems lost. If we open the "eyes" of our hearts, we will know the promise of hope that is one of Christ's greatest gifts.

Paul Pennick

THE FIRST GIFT

...for God is love. 1 John 4:8

"...God is love"—likely one of the most quoted phrases from the Bible—packs a profound truth. The *Catechism of the Catholic Church*, in paragraph 733, explains: "'God is Love' and love is his first gift, containing all others."

God loves you. God loves me. If we miss out on knowing this, we will miss much more besides. God's love for us is personal—the first gift he wishes us to accept from him.

Christmas offers us a season to reflect on this singular gift that sparks the abundance of all God's gifts. God's unfathomable love gives us Jesus, the Child of Bethlehem, born to save us. Love also sends the Spirit—and the Church—through which we have the Bible and sacraments and all the graces that flow to us through them. All are given by God so we might know this simple truth: God loves us.

Pat Gohn

Good Over Evil

**He heals the brokenhearted
and binds up their wounds.** Psalm 147:3

Through the ages, numerous people have searched for an answer
to a continuous modern problem. The brilliant philosophers and
theologians have tried to solve this puzzle under the title of theo-
dicy. That is a religious study that tries to reconcile the existence
of evil with the goodness of God. Innocent people suffer from
moral evils, becoming victims of anger, greed, violence and killing.
Others suffer from what are called physical evils: accidents and
catastrophes that may cause illness, injuries or death to innocent
victims. In both the moral and physical evils, we may become
bewildered because God does not stop these disasters. Jesus never
promised to cancel all evil. He said he would overcome evil. God's
love will be our hope and help. In Psalm 147, we are promised that
the goodness of God offers healing. When bad things happen to
good people, we don't understand. When good things happen to
good people, then we understand. In the final analysis, I trust that
the good will defeat the evil.

Fr. James McKarns

Seeking Him

Jesus turned and saw them following him and said to them, "What are you looking for?" They said to him, "Rabbi..., where are you staying?" John 1:38

I love how directly Jesus questions the disciples in this passage. He seems to be asking, "Just what is it you want from me?" Yet see how they sidestep his question? I wonder if they even knew what they were looking for. They were seekers, certainly. After all, they were following John the Baptist. Perhaps they felt some longing that they hoped Jesus could fulfill.

What is it that we are looking for when we turn to the Lord? When we lay our questions, sorrows and anger before him, what do we hope for in return? We may come to prayer hoping for guidance, comfort or even justice, but isn't it really Christ himself that we seek? Our desire for the Lord arises from God's own desire for us. We come to prayer to meet the Lord we long for, the Lord who sought us first, who is always with us.

Lord, it is you I seek!

Karla Manternach

Replacing Old Patterns

So whoever is in Christ is a new creation: the old things have passed away; behold, new things have come. 2 Corinthians 5:17

Many of us get stuck when it comes to New Year's resolutions, trying to use intention and willpower to make changes to old, ingrained habits. Rather than trying to change the old, Jesus calls us to take off the old and become the new. Instead of our own willpower, we have access to God's will and God's power. This is where true, lasting change occurs.

As a therapist, I view healing and change from a psycho-spiritual perspective, meaning that a client and I may have all the theory, intelligence and good intentions in the world, but we also must rely on the Holy Spirit guiding us and acting as the catalyst for change. In order to transcend ourselves, we need a power higher than ourselves.

What are the things you really want to change or release? What old patterns are you finally ready to replace? Where are you playing small, not rising to your full potential? Is this the year you become a new creation?

Lord, I am ready. Help me become who you want me to be.

Kristin Armstrong

Our Daily Epiphanies

You shall be radiant at what you see... Isaiah 60:5

Two people can experience the same event very differently. One might "see" God's hand at work while another may not. For example, one will curse his bad luck upon having a car accident, while the other will give thanks that God saved him from serious injury. In the end, some will have experienced their lives as a succession of little miracles, and they will count themselves blessed. Others will judge that life has been unfair and cheated them. The difference is typically in the eye of the beholder. If we have eyes to see the daily epiphanies in our lives, we will end up with grateful and joyful hearts. If we do not, we can easily become angry and dissatisfied. Let's begin this day with a prayer: "Lord, give me the eyes today and every day to see your generous and merciful hand at work." May every day be for us an epiphany of the Lord.

Msgr. Stephen J. Rossetti

LIVING IN JOY AND HOPE

Sing joyfully to the LORD, all you lands;
break into song; sing praise. Psalm 98:4

Shouting with joy, breaking into song and singing praise to the
Lord sounds like a great plan until I start listening to the news.
That's when I begin to falter. Reluctance sets in. I waver in the
midst of my joyful song. How does one pour joy into a world that
seems intent on spreading violence and hate? The world needs
our joy and hope. To pour our fear and anger into a world already
enslaved in fear and anger is not helpful. Starting today, let's watch
intently for good news. It, too, is all around us. It doesn't ordinar-
ily receive the coverage it deserves. The good that is being poured
out into the world is often overshadowed by the evil. Evil spelled
backward tells us to live. Let's find a way to live in joy and hope.

Sr. Macrina Wiederkehr, O.S.B.

Persistent Hope

...provided you persevere in the faith, firmly grounded, stable,
and not shifting from the hope of the Gospel that you heard...
Colossians 1:23

Sometimes it's easy to be a Christian. There's a whole lot of joy in a Baptism, Confirmation, wedding or ordination. There's a whole lot of spiritual healing in Confession and the Anointing of the Sick. As Catholics, we have the blessing of being fortified by the Eucharist at each and every Mass. And let's not forget about all those seemingly small but sacramental signs of God's love that we can see in our lives every day if we let ourselves. Other times, it's hard to be a Christian. We don't understand why God allows us, or those we love, to fall ill or why some in the world are hungry, troubled and oppressed. But being a Christian means we're in it for the long haul. We don't give up when our best-laid plans seem doomed to failure. We persist in hope because the Lord persists in love.

Jesus, thank you for the hope you bring to my life and to the world.

Melanie Rigney

He Is With Us

Do not let your hearts be troubled. John 14:1

So often in the last year, our hearts have been troubled. We continue to grieve our former lives. We are saddened by the loss of civility in our nation, by the loss of jobs and by the loss of loved ones. So much has changed so quickly in fundamental ways that have affected us all.

Yet Jesus assures us he is with us. He has not changed; he has never left us. We can count on him. His loving words to his disciples and to us are so full of tenderness and compassion, we cannot help but be comforted by them. In faith, we step out to embrace our changed lives, following his way, his truth and the new resurrected life he holds out to us. Whenever you feel confused, anxious or full of dismay, hear him speaking these words to you.

As the many parts of his Body here on earth, let us reassure one another with that same benevolence, that same steadfast love.

Jennifer Christ

No Matter What

I am convinced that neither death, nor life, nor angels, nor principalities…nor any other creature will be able to separate us from the love of God in Christ Jesus our Lord.

Romans 8:38-39

"Sister," bubbly nine-year-old Kayla blurted out, "once in God's family, you're in it for life. God loves us too much to let us go." We may become overwhelmed as we think of the hardest chapter in our life: the spiritual failures we wish had never happened, the unhealthy dependencies we cannot shake or the good things we fail to do. In these experiences, we may feel separated from the love of God. But St. Paul reminds us that God is there for us, no matter what. God helps us turn a new page, forgives our weaknesses with unconditional love, sets us free from our fetters and considers all the kindnesses we perform as done to Christ. Nothing in life—not the past, not the present, not things to come—can sever us from God's love. Assured of this, may we confidently go forward in hope, convinced that God loves us too much to ever let us go.

Sr. Bridget Haase, O.S.U.

Blanket of Promise

> Yet just as from the heavens
> > the rain and snow come down
> And do not return there
> > till they have watered the earth...
> So shall my word be...
> It shall not return to me empty... Isaiah 55:10, 11

The first time someone asked me to speak about the Bible for a weekend retreat, I laughed. Clearly, they had the wrong person or the wrong topic. Yet God was about to teach me otherwise. For as I prepared, God revealed how his Word had become an inherent part of my life. And speaking about it was a joy.

Like rain and snow, the heaven-sent words (from Mass, Old and New Testament readings, hymns and prayers) had seeped into my parched spirit. Almost unaware, I'd intrinsically embraced the Gospel stories as my own. *A father had two sons..., A woman touched the hem of his garment..., Do unto others...*

Even now, as steady flakes of snow blanket the ground, I cling to God's promise. Neither this snow, nor his Word, will return to him empty.

O Lord, our hope is in you, as you blanket us with your promise and water our souls.

Kathleen Swartz McQuaig

Embraced by God's Care

You are my shelter; from distress you will preserve me.

Psalm 32:7

Perhaps at some time or another, perhaps at this very moment, any one of us has been or is teetering on the edge of despair. So many of life's large challenges can root us in that terrible, frightening place: losing our job and finding no success despite our best efforts and constant searches for meaningful employment; struggling with ongoing, overwhelming depression; naming our inability to heal a cherished but fractured relationship; owning up to a pattern of flawed and imperfect choices. In such moments, the words of the psalmist encourage us to allow ourselves to be companioned in that prison of hopelessness by a loving God. This God has chosen for us the lot of truth, and that truth is emphatic: God's tender care for us endures no matter what is unfolding in our lives. We are God's beloved, and our days have meaning and purpose that endure beyond this current time and place.

Sr. Chris Koellhoffer, I.H.M.

The Faith of Friends

Many gathered together so that there was no longer room for them, not even around the door, and he preached the word to them… Unable to get near Jesus because of the crowd, they opened up the roof above him. Mark 2:2, 4

People are drawn inexorably to Jesus throughout the Gospel accounts. What motivates them? For some, undoubtedly, he was a curiosity. For others, hungering for hope, "he preached the word to them." For others, they were convinced that he was the best chance they had for healing.

What draws me to Jesus? Would I clamber up onto a rooftop for the sake of my paralyzed friend? Would I dig my way through the roof to get the attention of the rabbi? What would I say to him when our eyes meet?

Jesus sees the faith of these friends and commends them for putting it into action. They were willing to go the extra mile on faith and on friendship. As I follow Jesus more closely, may the Holy Spirit help me to be the one who helps another to find rest and healing in the Lord.

Steve Pable

My Source of Strength

**Be strong and take heart,
all who hope in the Lord.** Psalm 31:25

One of my uncles was fond of mumbling, "Give me strength!" under his breath when he was challenged by something...or someone. There are times when I find myself saying it before I can face leaving the house to start the day. Sometimes it takes strength to face the physical challenge of a storm, exhaustion from a bad night or some malady. Mostly, though, I find it's the interpersonal challenges of family, colleagues, students or the news that make me pray for strength.

The only source that can give me the strength is, indeed, hope in the Lord. The words of St. Julian of Norwich, "All shall be well, all shall be well, all manner of things shall be well," boost my hope at such times. To face the day, I sometimes hold these words in my heart as though clasping a medallion. With them, I do find the strength and courage to take heart and actually step out my door.

Aileen O'Donoghue

Turning to God

His heart was not entirely with the Lord, his God... 1 Kings 11:4

As a spiritual director, sometimes people tell me they cannot feel God's presence in their lives. They feel God is not "with them," even in prayer. I certainly understand these feelings, having had them myself. Indeed, how many of us go through life constantly aware of God's presence?

Living our lives in relationship with God is the story of our faith and, like all good stories, so much depends on the storyteller's point of view. For while we might fail to perceive God's presence— as have many holy men and women throughout time—the truth is that God is never not "with us." It is we who leave, we who are caught up in the busyness of our lives and forget that God is always standing next to us, awaiting our turning toward him to accept his embrace, like a patient, forgiving parent awaiting the return of the prodigal son or daughter.

God, turn me toward you so I can feel how close you are.

Steve Givens

FAITH AND HOPE

They that hope in the LORD will renew their strength...

Isaiah 40:31

The trees are once again barren in my area, and I know that it will be months before they display any outward signs of life. Like most people native to the northern part of our country, I may whine about the ice and snow, but I know from experience that someday spring will burst forth and the long cold winter days will be forgotten. There are seasons in our lives that feel like an endless winter. Illness, career uncertainty, financial problems and relationship troubles are just a few of the situations that challenge us. When I can let go of my demands and wait with an openhearted hope, I have a better chance of recognizing the answer to my prayer when it comes and even see how the unwelcome difficulties contributed to my growth.

God of infinite love and possibilities, help us to put our trust in you.

Terri Mifek

God Cares

The eyes of the Lord are upon those who fear him,
   upon those who hope for his kindness,
To deliver them from death
   and preserve them in spite of famine. Psalm 33:18-19

Our lives bring us many joys, but sometimes they also bring challenges that leave us anxious and confused. At such times, we know we need help, and the good news is that God wants to give it. This truth comes up again and again in Sacred Scripture. It seems God wanted to make sure that we got the point. When I reflect on how God has helped me through difficult times, I see that I never could have navigated successfully through the storms of life on my own. I see how God has shown me his care, and that brings hope for the future too. If God has been so good in the past, won't he be with me through all the challenges yet to come?

Lord, may the challenges of my life be catalysts for a greater trust in you.

Fr. Kenneth E. Grabner, C.S.C.

Leaning into Hope

**The light shines in the darkness,
and the darkness has not overcome it.** John 1:5

My gardening "skills" were limited to arranging silk flowers from the craft store. While my arrangements were uninspired, at least they wouldn't wither or die. My outlook changed during a winter that never seemed to end. Gloom settled into my soul, but how I wanted to lean into hope. An impulse to bring home a houseplant caught me off guard. Why would I do that to an innocent plant?

Despite my doubts, I purchased a tiny prayer plant. For the first time in a while, I felt hopeful. My plant wasn't showing any signs of withering. Each morning, it delighted me. Its leaves would stretch out as if welcoming the day. Each evening its leaves would fold up as if in prayer. I was fascinated with the wonder of it all. That prayer plant, so little, yet so resilient, inspired me to look beyond my own darkness to God's enduring light.

May we stretch out our hands each new day to God's goodness.

Gail Goleas

OUR HOPE RESTS IN JESUS

Remember Jesus Christ, raised from the dead, a descendant of David: such is my gospel, for which I am suffering, even to the point of chains, like a criminal. But the word of God is not chained. 2 Timothy 2:8-9

Certainly, the enemies of God would seek to limit the power of the Word by any means necessary, but sometimes even believers set out to micromanage the presence and action of God in the world. We imagine we know best who should and should not speak for the Lord, and just what they should say. And so we are tempted to use chains of sarcasm, threats and even physical force to constrain those whose religious expressions do not match our own. How foolish. If a religious impulse is from the Lord, no power on earth can stop it; if it is not from the Lord, it will fade away. Our task is to "remember Jesus Christ," as St. Paul says. All our hope rests upon our fidelity to him who has conquered the world.

Lord, help me to follow and trust you in all things.

Mark Neilsen

MAY GOD'S VISION OF ME BE MY VISION

The sins of my youth and my frailties remember not;
in your kindness remember me,
because of your goodness, O LORD. Psalm 25:7

A couple of my children are getting pretty old, which means that some memories of their childhood are more vivid than others. There are times in which one of my young adult sons will say to me, "Remember when I…" and they'll rattle off some offense they committed way back when.

Nope. More often than not, I don't remember. And even if I did, it wouldn't matter much. The past is over. It might impact the present, but I can't let it define it—for my sons or for myself, either.

I can't let myself be burdened by guilt over sins that I committed yesterday, sins that God has forgiven and for which I've been reconciled. I'm not going to define my children by things they did a decade ago. God doesn't define me that way, either. Isn't it time to let God's vision of me be my vision as well?

Forgiving God, release me from the chains of guilt and let me live in the present light of your love.

Amy Welborn

THE REALITY OF RESCUE

**When you pass through waters, I will be with you;
through rivers, you shall not be swept away.
When you walk through fire, you shall not be burned,
nor will flames consume you.** Isaiah 43:2

Many of life's crises have the power of a raging river to sweep us off our feet and into a whirlpool of doubt and distress. Sometimes, we may land in a situation that explodes like fire with anger or emotional pain. I've been stunned by such occurrences, so much so that I have had difficulty in knowing how to ask for God's help. The feeling of helplessness can be overwhelming. Then, a kind word from a friend or an offer from a stranger who promises to pray for me bring me back to an awareness that I am not alone in my heartache or grief. God's promise to rescue me becomes a reality. These moments encourage me to become more aware in times of struggle and in calm so that I may reach out to others in need and know that God is with us.

Deborah A. Meister

LOVING OUR ENEMIES

Love your enemies, and pray for those who persecute you, that you may be children of your heavenly Father, for he makes his sun rise on the bad and the good, and causes rain to fall on the just and the unjust. Matthew 5:44-45

I find it alarming how polarized we can be these days, politically in our nation and even within the Church. At all kinds of gatherings, anyone's remark may be a hot button that triggers listeners into seeing that person not only as wrong, but as a threat, an enemy. It can suddenly be hard to regard them lovingly.

What has helped me more than anything when I realize I am seeing someone as an enemy is to try to get out of the way so God could love them through me, praying: "Right now I can't seem to love them myself, any more than I can make the sun rise on them or the rain fall on them; but you can, Lord. Help me open myself to your love for them—and close my mouth."

Patricia Livingston

His Favorite

Do not fear, for I have redeemed you;
  I have called you by name: you are mine.
I give Egypt as ransom for you,
  Ethiopia and Seba in exchange for you.
Because you are precious in my eyes
  and honored, and I love you... Isaiah 43:1, 3-4

Years ago, my friend David was sharing a few words about the deeply personal love of the Lord, and he said something I'll never forget: "Jesus prefers your company." Despite our doubts or failings or feelings, at any given moment, Jesus wants to be with you more than anyone else.

He's never busy doing other things. He's never holding a grudge. He's never distracted by work or the worries of life. Jesus would like nothing more than to spend time with you. Today. He delights in being together. He looks forward to those moments as a highlight of his day. Your appointment time is circled on his calendar. Your artwork is hanging on his fridge. Your picture is in his wallet. His face lights up at the sound of your voice!

Steve Pable

Timeless Love

...because you loved me before the foundation of the world.

John 17:24

We are children of God, and God loved us long before we were born. I imagine God whispering to us just before we opened our eyes: "All that you will find easy, and all that you will find to be a burden and difficult, will all work together for your good because you are mine. You are a manifestation of my love. I have loved you from the beginning. I know you by name. Trust me to guide your path. Take courage."

As Jesus prayed for us, loved us and hoped for us to be one with him in God's love, each day we can lift our eyes in prayer and remember that God's love for us began long before this minute; it began before the foundation of the world.

Vivian Amu

THE GREAT APOSTLE

He said to them, "Go into the whole world and proclaim the gospel to every creature." Mark 16:15

If anyone went out into the "whole world," it was St. Paul. Today we celebrate the conversion of the apostle Paul, probably the Church's most ardent evangelist. He came to this vocation from an unlikely place. Known earlier as Saul of Tarsus, Paul was an aggressive persecutor of the fledgling Christian movement. After a divine encounter on the road to Damascus, he made an amazing transformation to become one of the most articulate leaders of the early Church. The spectacular growth of Christianity among the Gentiles of that time was due in large part to Paul's efforts. Despite considerable obstacles, his travels, writings and tireless work spread the faith.

From terrible sinner to saint, from persecutor to persuasive preacher, Paul gives us all hope: no matter what kind of life we have lived, we can change. Indeed, we can be welcomed back into the fold.

Paul Pennick

GRACE AT WORK

> When he arrived and saw the grace of God, he rejoiced and encouraged them all to remain faithful to the Lord in firmness of heart... Acts 11:23

What did Barnabas see when he arrived in Antioch? Just what does the grace of God look like? I suspect, for many of us, the grace of God is difficult to define and categorize but fairly easy to recognize when it makes an appearance. Hopefully we have seen it embodied and at work countless times in the lives of family, friends, coworkers and, yes, ourselves. When we witness patterns of generous and gracious living, quiet acts of thoughtfulness, tender care for the wounds of one's neighbor, time given over to contemplation and reflection, the selfless sharing of one's attention and energy for the common good, we see what Barnabas was looking at and what caused him to rejoice: the Kingdom of God unfolding. Today may we look for and find signs of the grace of God at work all around us in our world.

Sr. Chris Koellhoffer, I.H.M.

Holding Fast to Hope

We who have taken refuge might be strongly encouraged to hold fast to the hope that lies before us. This we have as an anchor of the soul, sure and firm... Hebrews 6:18-19

During the recent pandemic years, we learned what it really means to seek refuge. We stayed home and tried to find hope and security there while we waited. We had fewer options, but we always had a choice: We could look forward with hope or throw in the towel.

God calls us to live always in hope, whether in the hope of a better world now or in the promise of eternal life. That hope is not always easy to come by. We can lose our grip when we get tossed about on the deck of a ship in a roiling sea. We can even get thrown overboard. And yet, even there we might find an anchor waiting, "sure and firm." The perils of life will always be, but so, too, the steadfastness of God.

Be my anchor in the storm, my God.

Steve Givens

Quietly Preparing

He is like a tree
   planted near running water,
That yields its fruit in due season... Psalm 1:3

In thinking of the lessons I have learned in life, my parents come first to mind, followed by many teachers. Another "teacher" I can count on is my "other mother"—the Earth. I have found that by quieting myself and looking deeply—listening to nature, if you will—powerful bits of wisdom may be gleaned.

Trees are marvelous teachers. Watching those fall leaves twirl to the ground, I'm invited to ask, "What am I hanging on to?" This can be an eye opener!

I think particularly of a tree in winter. What courage it takes to stand bare before the world, its scars clearly revealed. What do I learn? That healing can happen. Most of all, I learn from trees not to give up hope. Although they may look lifeless in winter, they are merely quietly preparing to come forth when the weather warms to once again bear fruit. Like love that is said to never fail, a tree reminds us that hope, too, springs eternal.

May I learn to listen with the ears and eyes of the heart, Beloved, for it is there I learn to hope.

Judy Schueneman

Resting in God's Will

Why are you terrified, O you of little faith? Matthew 8:26

The apostles lost control of their boat in the storm, and though things looked hopeless, Christ had his hand over them. I tend to be in control or else flying off the handle. As long as I'm running the show, I'm a happy person. Take away my power, and I become anxious and fretful. Pride convinces us that we control our circumstances, and when we lose control, that is when we tend to feel fear. The humble man fears nothing. Control is a temporary illusion, but God is good, and he alone is God. God always has us in hand, and we can trust that all things work for the good—the beginnings of life and its end, our triumphs and our failures. There is no reason a Christian should succumb to anxiety about the future, about death, about politics or the economy. Christ's victory over evil is assured. Let's pray for the humility to rest confidently, courageously, in his will.

Elizabeth Duffy

OUR BIG GOD

They forgot the God who had saved them,
who had done great deeds in Egypt... Psalm 106:21

When I am faced with an obstacle or situation that looms large before me, I can measure myself against it and lose heart. When I feel myself shrinking, I need the reminder that God is Big. It's nice to have a friend or family member take hold of me and remind me. It's even better when I remember how to remind myself.

How many times has God saved me? *Every. Single. Time.*

Then out loud, or on paper if it helps me to see ink on the page as proof, I list all the times God has come through for me or for the people I love. Every time I thought there was no answer and he answered me or gave me new questions. Every time I thought I was out of options and he opened an unseen path before me. Every time I thought I would fall apart and he held me together. Every time I thought I wasn't enough and he showed me that with him, I was. Every time I was inconsolable and he consoled me.

Remember.

Kristin Armstrong

Turn to Jesus

I do believe, help my unbelief! Mark 9:24

One of the most recognized lines from the Scriptures comes from the father who brought his possessed son to Jesus to be healed. Jesus chides him for his lack of faith, whereupon the father responds, "I do believe, help my unbelief!"

We can relate to this man's desperation and to his weak faith. In life, there are frequent reminders of our lack of faith. As a priest, I, too, know my faith should be stronger and that I could move mountains if only my faith were the size of a mustard seed. Yet it is not. Instead of giving up and losing hope, we ought to be like this father who, despite his lack of faith, cried out to the Lord for help. His prayer was heard. We, too, know our faith is weak. But Jesus hears us in our weakness. He hears even the faintest of our cries, and he will answer us.

Msgr. Stephen J. Rossetti

Thank God Ahead

> Brothers and sisters: Have no anxiety at all, but in everything, by prayer and petition, with thanksgiving, make your requests known to God. Then the peace of God that surpasses all understanding will guard your hearts and minds in Christ Jesus.
>
> Philippians 4:6-7

I'm not going to lie. In the wake of the coronavirus pandemic of 2020, like many, my own anxieties escalated concerning the needs of my family and my work and more. Daily, I would go to prayer: "in everything, by prayer and petition."

Yes, God hears my petitions. I trust in it. Yet Paul's Letter offers an additional insightful instruction for these petitions—to offer them "with thanksgiving." This might seem startling at first. But ultimately, I find it consoling. To give thanks alongside my petitions follows the counsel of many saints, that is, to thank God *ahead* of time. We may not have answers yet to these heartfelt prayers...yet we're to be grateful for God's providence in the *now*.

This is more than just looking on the bright side of things. This is how a living faith leads us to peace, by uniting our hearts and minds daily with Christ.

Lord, into your mighty hands, I place all my cares.

Pat Gohn

Light in Little Things

You are the light of the world. Matthew 5:14

Many of us can sing or hum the hope-filled hymn, "This Little Light of Mine." Jesus did not challenge us to be neon signs or vibrant flashing billboards. He said that we are to let *our* light shine.

Margaret Silf, in her book *Compass Points*, reflects upon her first trip to New York and the late-night ride to the viewing platform of the Empire State Building. There she gazed upon a breathtaking vista of lights. Silf remarks that the beauty was not due to some lavish Hollywood show—it was the result of millions of people switching on the lights in their homes.

This is how we are to be...be it as a community of fireflies, a bright flashlight or a flickering candle. Do we bring hope—or increase the darkness by being people of gloom and doom? Let us be people of light who know that only the light of God can conquer the darkness and not allow it to prevail.

Gracious God, let light shine in and through me.

Sr. Bridget Haase, O.S.U.

HOPE IS ALWAYS JUSTIFIED

One man was there who had been ill for thirty-eight years.

John 5:5

Thirty-eight years, in the time of Jesus, was a good long time, way more than half of a lifetime. John's Gospel doesn't tell us how old the man was when he became ill, but chances are he had been afflicted since he was a youth. But the man evidently has never given up hope, even after thirty-eight years. He still hopes for healing, and he doesn't merely lie around home, whatever it may be, waiting for healing. No. He has gone to the trouble to get from wherever he lives to the pool called Bethesda. There he hopes to find healing. Can you imagine how many times, over the course of thirty-eight years, this man was tempted to despair? Maybe he even did despair sometimes. But if he ever felt like giving up, later he chose to embrace hope again. No matter how grim things may look right now, hope is always justified.

Lord Jesus, help me to embrace hope at all times and in all circumstances.

Mitch Finley

Remembering God's Blessings

However, take care and be earnestly on your guard not to forget the things which your own eyes have seen, nor let them slip from your memory... Deuteronomy 4:9

Psychologists say that we humans are capable of selective retention. This means that, to a certain extent, we can pick and choose those things we wish to remember and those we wish to forget. Selective retention comes in handy at times. It helps us not to dwell on all our negative experiences. It can also help us to remember some of the good things we have experienced. Some negative experiences we cannot forget, and that's all right. Such experiences hopefully have taught us valuable lessons and helped us to grow in wisdom, compassion and trust in God. In the passage above, Moses instructs the people always to remember the good things God has done for them. So must we.

A suggestion: Take a few minutes today to remember three ways God has blessed you and your life.

God, may I always remember you are with me in good times and in bad. Today, I thank you especially for_____.

Sr. Melannie Svoboda, S.N.D.

Guiding Light

**Send forth your light and your fidelity;
they shall lead me on...** Psalm 43:3

On a trip to Hawaii, my husband and I went on a guided hike through a rain forest. We crossed gushing streams, climbed a sheer cliff and trudged through thick mud. But along the way, we saw incredible beauty and an amazing diversity of plant life. Although more challenging than I had anticipated, it was a great experience largely because we had a knowledgeable guide who struck just the right balance of patience and encouragement.

As we face the various trials that are an inevitable part of life, we can become overwhelmed. Sometimes the negative forces in and around us threaten to overshadow all that is good and beautiful in ourselves and the world. During those times, it is imperative to trust the still small voice of the Spirit. Like any good guide, that voice will use healthy doses of patience and encouragement to move us along the path of faith, hope and love.

Terri Mifek

Priorities

Some ignored the invitation and went away, one to his farm, another to his business. Matthew 22:5

I'm one of those people who not only makes to-do lists, but who also makes lists of her lists. There's the grocery list, the day job list, the writing list, the reading list and so on. Lists aren't inherently bad; they can help keep us organized and on track.

But to-do lists can be deadly to our souls, if we are more devoted to them than we are to God. In this Gospel verse, we hear about guests who turned aside the invitation to the Lord's feast because their earthly work was their priority. The next time you begin a list or review an existing one, make worship and openness to grace the most important item, not a "nice to have if there's time after everything else is done."

God, may the activities that populate my schedule be informed by my time with you.

Melanie Rigney

Trust That God Will Answer

He was amazed at their lack of faith. Mark 6:6

Jesus was visiting his relatives and neighbors, and you would think this would have been an ideal time for him to offer his gift of healing. But there was a serious problem! Many did not believe that Jesus could do anything for them, and so he could help only a few. He was amazed at their lack of faith. This story shows us that there is no healing without faith. There has to be an openness and a desire for the healing power of Jesus.

I think faith includes the trust that God will answer our prayers for healing in the way that is best for us, but that might not eliminate all of our sorrows. Jesus lived a life of love that had both joys and sorrows, and his final suffering gave way to resurrection. Jesus said to us, "Follow me." If we follow, then his pathway will be ours. May this hope bring us peace.

Fr. Kenneth E. Grabner, C.S.C.

In the Silence

I have stilled and quieted
my soul like a weaned child. Psalm 131:2

How difficult this is to do—and how crucial. Once, I went with a parish group to a retreat at a monastery. When we arrived and went to our rooms, I was astonished to realize it would be three days of total silence—no talking, no engagement with each other, no media. What? I went to my room furious! Alone in the silence. How could they expect this? Soon enough, I discovered plenty of noise and chatter inside my head: complaints, criticisms, bitterness, regrets, self-doubts, old hurts and plenty more, jostling and shoving for attention. The silence itself taught me to let go of the inner clutter and find beneath it a space, a quiet I'd never encountered before. My soul became still like the water on the lake in the early morning. And in the silence, I knew…I was not alone.

Dear God, in your silence, teach me to know you, to rejoice in hope, endure in affliction and persevere in prayer.

Mary Marrocco

Avoiding Collisions

...that you, rooted and grounded in love, may have strength to comprehend...the breadth and length and height and depth, and to know the love of Christ...so that you may be filled with all the fullness of God. Ephesians 3:17-19

To avoid aircraft collisions, cell towers over 200 feet are required to have red and white blinking lights. When a bulb burns out, a radio tower climber scales up the structure to change it with nothing but a safety harness. Some towers are as high as 1,700 feet. Can you imagine?

Each of us is susceptible to our own burnout when we don't stay connected to God as our power source. As hope flickers and fades, our risk of colliding with despair increases. Fortunately, we have God's love to recharge us. The more we ground ourselves in it, the greater the depth and height of our hope. With God as our safety harness, the sky's the limit!

Source of All, keep my hope constantly energized so it burns bright for you.

Claire McGarry

WATERING THE GARDEN

**He will renew your strength,
and you shall be like a watered garden...** Isaiah 58:11

In the middle of a harsh Wisconsin winter, this is truly good news! About now I find myself weary of boots, scarves, itchy hats and too much indoors. To be like a watered garden! I surely need the refreshment and renewal God promises! Glossy garden books, the first seed catalogs in my mailbox, even the pictures of last year's flowers on my computer hold the promise of the green lushness I begin to crave by mid-February. I hope, trust and believe with unshaken certainty that spring will come, as it has every year. God desires abundance for us. He set the first of our kind to live in a garden so stunningly beautiful and harmonious it was called Paradise. The sorrow, the losses, the diminishments, the grief of our present life will be healed! We will be renewed and strengthened by his mercy, and we will reside in the eternal abundance of his love.

Lord, you are the source of my refreshment! I open my parched soul to your life-giving water.

Jennifer Christ

What We Need

**Behold, thus is the man blessed
who fears the Lord.** Psalm 128:4

A number of years ago, a priest friend and I took a woman suffering from terminal cancer to Lourdes. She was not Catholic but willingly came along. When we arrived, she plunged into the waters and joined us in prayer. Sometime later, she died.

Before she passed, she said to me, "I am glad I went to Lourdes." It was clear that she received a special grace, although not a physical healing as we had hoped.

So many people become angry when they do not get what they want from God. I think it best to repeat the phrase, "God gives us what we need, not what we want."

I believe this woman died in gratitude and hope. God answered her prayers. God answers our prayers. We, too, should be grateful and live, and die, in hope.

Msgr. Stephen J. Rossetti

OUR DESIRE FOR GOD

Your Father knows what you need before you ask him.

Matthew 6:8

So then, you may ask yourself, what is the point of prayer? If God already knows what I need, why should I bother to ask him? God wants connection with his children. He values the relationship even more than we value his response to our needs. He wants to hear our voices and sense our dependence on his strength. He wants our petitions and our praise to be a continuing conversation throughout our lives.

Besides, God in his infinite wisdom knows that we are often confused. When we talk things over with him in prayer, the Holy Spirit enlightens us in the conversation. As our layers peel back, our vulnerability is exposed. The light of the divine filters in, and we begin to see that perhaps we are asking for the wrong things. Gently, through relationship, God aligns our hearts with his purposes, and our prayers become echoes in the hallways of heaven. Our needs are met, yes, but more importantly, our deepest longing is addressed—our desire for God.

Kristin Armstrong

That You Have Chosen Me

I have called you friends... It was not you who chose me, but I who chose you. John 15:15, 16

Of the many passages in Scripture revealing God's love for us, this one stands out in a special way for me. That Jesus chooses us, and that what he chooses us for is to be a friend, I find an astonishing revelation. The relationship of friend is much more personal than just a follower or believer. It suggests warm, valued mutuality.

Real friendship comes from an ongoing sharing of life, both profound and lighthearted, in which we have come to know each other deeply. We have been together in emergency rooms and surprise birthday parties. Spending time together matters to us greatly.

Jesus, that you have chosen me for your own friend, inviting me to share your life as you share mine, is a precious window on your love. When I struggle to pray sometimes, if I remember you as friend, I feel myself relax. I can just spend time with you wherever I am right then.

Patricia Livingston

Grasping God's Hand

For I am the LORD, your God,
who grasp your right hand. Isaiah 41:13

My wife and I have been holding hands for more than 35 years, and I can still remember being a slightly scared teenager reaching for her hand for the first time.

For many young people, holding hands is their first experience of intimacy. Before a first kiss, before even a chaste hug, almost always comes the simple act of holding hands. In that grasp, perhaps, lies the foundation of the most sacramental of relationships.

That God reaches out and desires to be in relationship with us is the greatest mystery of our lives. God desires this relationship but never demands it. Instead, God "comes courting," quietly making his presence known in our lives and waiting for us to respond. When we turn toward God, our life of faith begins. When we accept God's offer of life and love, we are converted and transformed, our lives never again the same because the Creator of all holds our hands.

Lord, draw me into a life with you.

Steve Givens

APPROVAL RATINGS

...no prophet is accepted in his own native place. Luke 4:24

In this chapter of Luke's Gospel, Jesus' approval rating plummets. The hometown crowd, convinced they know exactly who Jesus is and where he comes from, cannot accept that he is anything more. Still, our Lord offers a powerful response: Jesus doesn't try to change the crowd's presuppositions that blind them to greater possibilities. He knows their hearts. He acknowledges their skepticism, speaks truth and moves on. Critics cannot define him—nor derail his mission.

I appreciate Jesus' approach in the face of rejection. Worth isn't measured by community acceptance or mass appeal. Popular opinion doesn't dictate one's identity. Rather, Jesus calls each of us to a particular mission with unique talents. So instead of letting feeble presumptions stifle us, let's affirm our mission and apply our God-given gifts. Our inherent approval rating from God is what truly matters.

Lord, please help us remember it is you who commissions us, and it is your acceptance that matters.

Kathleen Swartz McQuaig

Waiting Together

**My soul waits for the Lord
more than sentinels wait for the dawn.** Psalm 130:6

Psalm 130 is a lament often used in liturgical prayers for loved ones who have died. It speaks of the depths of profound sorrow and overwhelming grief in which we sometimes find ourselves. But it's not without hope, even at our lowest times. However long the night, the psalmist sings, we wait in the company of a God who never abandons, a faithful companion to us. We wait with hearts aware and attentive as a sentinel, watching for the first sign of dawn. We wait for the daylight in hope that it will break through our loss and pain. That's a whole lot of waiting, but we do not wait alone. The Holy One waits with us.

Sr. Chris Koellhoffer, I.H.M.

Unyielding Faith

O woman, great is your faith! Matthew 15:28

The Canaanite woman begging Jesus to exorcise her daughter in this Gospel story was likely a pagan. Yet she has seemingly come to faith in Jesus as the Messiah. To onlookers, her proclamation of faith would have been most unexpected—and it seems to even take Jesus by surprise.

Jesus is won over by her unyielding display of faith. And he grants her request, and her daughter is healed instantly.

The woman's faith and persistence show us the posture we ought to have in prayer: Go to Jesus. Pursue him, even. Trust and believe.

What do I need to bring to Jesus, in faith, right now?

Pat Gohn

A New Dawn

God called the light "day," and the darkness he called "night." Evening came, and morning followed—the first day.

Genesis 1:5

God created our world out of nothing, starting with light. What we can observe with the most powerful telescope or a microscope of the highest resolution reveals only a fraction of God's creative power. Every time we pray the Glory Be, we remind ourselves of God's enduring power, poured out in love "as it was in the beginning, is now, and shall be forever." Into our darkest moments of crisis, God will bring forth a new dawn. People of hope stand in the darkness faithfully trusting in God's promise to bring light even though it seems most impossible.

God of all creation, I believe you are at work in me through the Holy Spirit to be a sign of your great love for this world.

Deborah A. Meister

HE'S GOT THE POWER

You come against me with sword and spear and scimitar, but
I come against you in the name of the LORD of hosts...

1 Samuel 17:45

When faced with Goliath, I doubt David said, "Hey, I'm pretty
good with a slingshot. I'll take a shot at this guy." Instead, I suspect
he somehow found within himself evidence of God's protection.
He might have remembered past experiences of God's care. Maybe
when Samuel anointed him, David became assured of God's presence within him.

However it happened, David seems full of confidence in this
battle scene. That he was obviously overmatched reveals his faith in
God's care. That victory came is a cause for hope for all of us who
face long odds. Though we might be defenseless, God is always
dominant.

Are you facing an enemy? May you, like David, find courage
within yourself and confidence in God's care.

Julia DiSalvo

Mission Impossible?

...if one has a grievance against another; as the Lord has forgiven you, so must you also do. Colossians 3:13

My son and I attended a recital of organ students. He—who'd just begun lessons—was supposed to be inspired, but instead teetered on the edge of despair. "I'll never be able to do that," he moaned. I reminded him of all the other things that had once seemed impossible but that he'd now mastered. I could make my own lifelong list: reading books without pictures, algebra—how can you do math with letters?—birthing and raising children, writing a whole book, getting through the day of my husband's funeral. And forgiveness. Always forgiveness. Considered from both ends—extending and receiving forgiveness—it can seem an impossible place to reach: Will they ever forgive me? Can I ever forgive them? But, trusting and imitating the Teacher and reflecting on the stories of mercy reflected in the lives of those who've practiced what he taught, I can see that, no, it's not impossible at all.

Amy Welborn

GOD REALLY CARES FOR ME

Cast all your worries upon him because he cares for you.

1 Peter 5:7

My first day on retreat, I spotted an ant on the sidewalk carrying a leaf many times his size. As I watched him struggling, I found myself saying to him, "I know just how you feel, buddy!" My spontaneous response to that little ant spoke volumes to me about where I was physically, spiritually and psychologically that particular day.

Paying attention to our spontaneous thoughts, feelings and words is a good way to begin to pray. Once we know where we are, we can begin to compare that with where we would like to be. Then we can pray for those graces we need to get there. If I'm crabby, for example, I may need the grace of patience, rest or gratitude. If I'm lonely, I may need to reach out to a friend or to someone in need. If I feel overburdened, I may need to renew my trust in the God who really, really cares for me.

Loving and caring God, help me to begin my prayer today by telling you where I am.

Sr. Melannie Svoboda, S.N.D.

The Great Joy in Trust and Hope

For I know well the plans I have in mind for you—oracle of the Lord—plans for your welfare and not for woe, so as to give you a future of hope. Jeremiah 29:11

A friend of mine, abandoned by her parents while she was in high school, was living in her car. She was pregnant. Today, thirty years later, happily married with a beautiful home and two adult children, she says it was Jeremiah 29:11 that got her through that awful time. It gets her through today's challenges—the loss of friends and relatives, health issues and the other confusion that besets all of us here on earth.

Believing in that future of hope can set our weary minds at rest as well. We don't have to do it alone, not pregnant teenagers living in their cars, not single women in positions of corporate or governmental power, not moms scrambling for ways to keep their families fed. He has loving plans for us, and if we listen carefully, he will guide us to fulfilling them.

Thank you, Father, for loving me.

Melanie Rigney

God's Healing Power

For the Lord hears the poor,
and his own who are in bonds he spurns not. Psalm 69:34

If you or someone you love feels weak, trapped, unworthy or hopeless today, this verse is sent for our healing. Just when we think we are least deserving, God wants us to know that we deserve his love. Just when we feel tethered to our sin or handcuffed to our unpleasant circumstances, God wants us to know that for as bad as we feel, he has plans for our good. Just when we are at our worst, God shows up with his best. It's the infallible gift for a failing heart.

Pour your heart out to God today, on behalf of your personal needs or on behalf of the needs of someone you love. Take divine comfort in knowing that he hears you, and he is already working behind the scenes to remedy difficult circumstances. Confess your weakness and need to the one true source of all help. Trust that he will show up for you in mighty and inexplicable ways.

Kristin Armstrong

CREDIT FOR GOOD INTENTIONS

For I do not do the good I want, but I do the evil I do not want.

Romans 7:19

We can all reflect how we have often tried to improve in some area of our lives only to fall back into our former ways. Giving up the habit of smoking or remaining faithful to a healthy eating program, for example. Our good intentions are often and easily defeated by old bad habits that continue to pull us down. I think we often fail to improve because we are unwilling to endure the suffering required to make the transition to a better way of life. St. Paul confesses his weakness in doing the very things he resolved he would not do. Our New Year's resolutions are often soon forgotten, and our Lenten promises can disappear about as quickly as the ashes on our foreheads. I know I am not the person that the Lord would expect me to be. But my hope is that God, who knows our hearts and understands our desires, will at least give me credit for having good intentions and making a continual effort to improve.

Fr. James McKarns

GRACE IN HARD TIMES

But now…do not reproach yourselves for having sold me here. It was really for the sake of saving lives that God sent me here ahead of you. Genesis 45:5

How many of us, like Joseph, can look back on difficult times and see them as part of a bigger picture? Job loss can open new opportunities. A breakup can lead to new love. That doesn't mean we would choose them. If I could go back and stop the COVID-19 pandemic, I would absolutely prevent the loneliness, loss and conflict of that time. However, I also see the grace embedded in it. When my family could no longer gather, we kept in closer contact than ever. When my children couldn't see friends, they grew closer to each other. We experienced fresh longing for the Eucharist, felt greater gratitude for our blessings and found new ways to care for one another. God was with us through it all, shining light in the darkness.

Lord, when darkness falls, help me to look for your light!

Karla Manternach

Follow Our Leader

Whoever wishes to come after me must deny himself, take up his cross, and follow me. Matthew 16:24

Spiritual director Lyn tells the story of her grandson. Alex loved to make swords out of aluminum foil. Lyn grabbed a fake sword and shouted, "Let's head for the kitchen and the monster behind the door." Alex led the way. At the door, he turned to Lyn and said, "Nana, I got a great idea. You go first."

We all have crosses that Jesus asks us to actively embrace, to take up, not just to passively accept and then to follow him in hope. He has gone first. He leads us and shows us how to suffer. We begin Lent with the Sign of the Cross; we enter a church or begin our prayer with this same sign.

May the Cross be a reminder to follow our leader.

Sr. Bridget Haase, O.S.U.

We Are Not Alone

Many are saying of me,
  "There is no salvation for him in God."
But you, O Lord, are my shield. Psalm 3:3-4

The psalmist's adversaries wield words. They tell him his situation is hopeless. This is a powerful weapon—to get people to abandon hope: "You can't do this with your own resources, and there's nothing else, so you might as well give up." We hear it all the time. We face the taunting temptation to believe that we are all alone and shouldn't even bother to seek help. But the psalmist looks to what he knows. He knows that when he prays, he feels God listening. He knows that when he sleeps, he wakes again; he is sustained. So he fears not. Like the psalmist, let us not believe the lie but instead reassure ourselves daily, based on the evidence, that we are not alone, that God—in our hearts and acting through others—upholds us.

Phil Fox Rose

THE INFINITE LOVE OF GOD

It had already grown dark, and Jesus had not yet come to them. John 6:17

When a friend lost both of her parents in a car accident, she was understandably devastated. Although many people offered words of consolation, she told me nothing brought her peace until one woman silently held her in her arms and allowed her to cry. She said that was the moment when she was first able to feel the compassion of God. Whether in our personal lives or in the larger community, there will be times when we will sit in the darkness of fear, anger, depression or disillusionment. When we are near our breaking point, faith in the infinite love of God helps us understand that we are not alone in our suffering. God's love gives us the hope that resurrection was not a one-time event, but a pattern of how God brings new life out of situations that appear hopeless.

Terri Mifek

THE 'CELEBRITIES' IN GOD'S KINGDOM

> [Jesus said:] "Not everyone who says to me, 'Lord, Lord,' will enter the kingdom of heaven, but only the one who does the will of my Father in heaven." Matthew 7:21

We are a celebrity-crazed society. Whether the celebrity is an actor, singer, sports figure, politician, religious leader or other achiever, we hold that person in awe. Even in the smaller circles where we spend our daily lives, there are "celebrities." Jesus tells us, however, that all that really matters is doing God's will.

For some, doing God's will catapults them into celebrity status on earth. Most of us are called to do things that may not garner us accolades or awards but that contribute significantly to spreading God's love in this world. God puts no value on our status in this world or on the earthly treasure we accumulate. Jesus came to call us to love God and one another. Regardless of our status or lot in life, this is all that matters. What greater role is there than to be God's messenger of faith, love and hope?

Charlotte A. Rancilio

The Bottom Line

Paul...Apostle of Jesus Christ for the sake of the...recognition of religious truth, in the hope of eternal life... Titus 1:1

I decided to take a walk outside in the early hours of one morning as the sun was just rising. Still darkened against a sky only beginning to reflect the light of dawn, the trees rustled in the breeze, and I was moved by the beauty of it all. I could sense the presence of God breathing life into the new day. Quietly I stopped in gratitude. Ah, I thought. Even if those who claim to be atheists sometimes prevail in politics, public policy or culture, they still have no choice but to live in a world that exists as the consequence of a Creator who makes us, a world that has been redeemed by Christ. No one can escape this because it is simply true. Like Paul, we religious sisters dedicate ourselves to living so intensely that those who wish to see truth can see it, attracted by the beauty of lives that manifest the mystery that we are eternally loved. For I believe even atheists hope, somewhere in their heart of hearts, for a life without end.

Sr. Kathryn James Hermes, F.S.P.

Trusting in Redemption

Into your hands I commend my spirit. Psalm 31:6

In Luke's passion account, we hear these words from Jesus just before he dies. For years I have used a form of those words at the center of my prayer, commending into God's hands whatever is in my heart. I never realized Jesus' words were from Psalm 31:6, the first of its two lines. One Holy Week, someone I love greatly was on the edge of death. I had just enough time between hospital visits to go to a service. The psalm printed in the program was Psalm 31. We recited together: "Into your hands I commend my spirit." The next words of the psalm practically shone on the page for me: "You will redeem me, O Lord, O faithful God." I felt a huge surge of joyful hope. Jesus knew this psalm; he knew the rest of this verse. His prayer was more than resigned surrender; it was absolute trust that redemption and new life was just ahead.

Faithful God, what a gift to know your redeeming love is right here.

Patricia Livingston

NOT ALONE IN MY SORROW

**Another is a friend, a boon companion,
who will not be with you when sorrow comes.** Sirach 6:10

I have been blessed throughout my life with friends who are not just companions, but spiritual sisters. At this time in our lives, when many of us are married with children and have numerous duties of our own, it's difficult to find time for enjoyment of one another's company. All the more so, our own duties can be so weighted and binding that serving one another in significant and physical ways is just not possible. But my friends provide something that is still valuable in my times of struggle—that is, shared hope and longing for our Creator and Jesus, his Son. In our times of distress, our temptation can be to despair, to lose sight of the love of God. Sometimes, even though they can't lift my physical burdens for me, just hearing my friends say, "I am with you in the struggle and I love you," is enough to remind me of the presence of God in my sorrow.

Elizabeth Duffy

FAITH GIVES MEANING TO OUR LIVES

He believed, hoping against hope, that he would become "the father of many nations," according to what was said, "Thus shall your descendants be." Romans 4:18

St. Paul is talking about the faith of Abraham, a man who was quite old and childless when God promised that he would be the father of many nations. Abraham had no material evidence to support this promise, but he had the faith to believe that God would do what he said. Abraham's faith was a gift of God that brought meaning to his life.

God has made promises to us too. He promised to help us in our difficulties and to be with us in a special way through his sacraments. And he promised us the gift of resurrection. We have no material evidence for these promises, but we have our faith that gives us the intuition that God's promises are true. Faith is the gift of God that brings us hope and joy. Without faith, we cannot find the meaning in our lives that God wants us to have.

Lord, increase my faith.

Fr. Kenneth E. Grabner, C.S.C.

Loving God Despite the Suffering

Paul and Silas were praying and singing hymns to God as the prisoners listened... Acts 16:25

Paul is the poster child for suffering. He endured much for his faith—as he himself took pains to report. In this passage alone, we see Paul stripped, beaten, imprisoned and bound to a stake. And what is he doing in the midst of it all? He is praying! He is *singing*! Even the earthquake that opens his cell is less surprising than his tranquility in the face of his own hardship.

There was a time in my life when I believed I had to go looking for suffering in order to be closer to Jesus. I thought that pain would teach me about the Cross, so I sought it out. Now I understand that we all suffer. The challenge is to accept the suffering that comes to us with as much grace as we can. Like Paul, who makes no attempt to escape from hardship even when the opportunity arises, I think our task is to remain grateful to God in spite of it.

Lord God, my life is sometimes hard, but all that I have is from you. Thank you.

Karla Manternach

An Act of Trust

The Lord is my shepherd; I shall not want. Psalm 23:1

The COVID-19 pandemic has devastated lives on so many levels. We mourn the collective loss of life and the empty places at the table. Many of us also grieve the abrupt termination of employment that supported us and our way of life. A friend let go by the restaurant industry told me that she often lay awake at night in terror over what might happen to her and her family without the needed income generated by her job. Her list of "What if?" questions fueled a mounting anxiety. As she searched for peace, this verse from Psalm 23 became her prayer. Over and over, she uttered it as an act of trust in God's promise.

What a challenge to believe that, even when the landscape around us is shifting and uncertain, there is nothing we lack. Nothing. As we walk the Lenten journey with the Holy One beside us, still waters, green pastures, the restoring of our soul—these are all promised by a God who does not abandon.

Holy One, shepherd me with your love.

Sr. Chris Koellhoffer, I.H.M.

VINDICATION FOR THE JUST

If the just one be the son of God, he will defend him and deliver him from the hand of his foes. Wisdom 2:18

Isn't this what we all want to believe: that if a person is doing what God wants, he or she will be protected from harm, especially from the wickedness of other people? But our experience tells us that isn't so. And it wasn't so for Jesus himself. The thinking expressed in this passage from the Book of Wisdom reflects a misunderstanding of what it means for God to care for us. Those who think this way know "not the hidden counsels of God" (Wisdom 2:22). From the perspective of this brief life on earth, the just one's fate seems tragic, even pointless. But viewed from the eternal love of God, there is reward and vindication for the righteous. That is our hope, a hope that is beyond the schemes and calculations of worldly wisdom.

Jesus, strengthen my faith in your eternal care for me and those I love.

Mark Neilsen

THE ULTIMATE SACRIFICE

> **Behold, we are going up to Jerusalem, and the Son of Man will be handed over to the chief priests and the scribes, and they will condemn him to death, and hand him over to the Gentiles to be mocked and scourged and crucified, and he will be raised on the third day.** Matthew 20:18-19

Jesus' torture, crucifixion and death changed the world forever. This is the story of Lent, the story of our faith. That sacrifice by Jesus saved us from sin and gave us the gift of eternal life. He taught us to love our enemies as he loved those who crucified him. He taught us to pray as he prayed for his torturers. He taught us to deny ourselves simple pleasures so that we can focus on our spiritual journey. He taught us to love the poor, to care for those less fortunate. He changed the world with his message of love, mercy and forgiveness. He died for our sins. We live in hope because of his sacrifice.

Paul Pennick

GOD'S PROMISE

Lo, I am about to create new heavens
and a new earth...
No longer shall the sound of weeping be heard there,
or the sound of crying. Isaiah 65:17, 19

We undertook this Lenten journey because we want to be closer to God and each other, and closer to our own true selves. The way can be costly and humbling, though. It's hard to face our sins and failings—the big ones we know cause harm, the habitual ones that seem to erode our souls—and harder still to overcome them. Like the first gentle spring breeze when winter seemed bitterly relentless, these words of Isaiah come. They bring hope. They remind us it is not our work. We do not have to re-create ourselves. It is God's promise, God's faithful action in our lives, that makes the impossible real. In Christ, the healing presence of God among us.

Thank you, dear God, for bringing joy where there are tears, and healing where there is hurt.

Mary Marrocco

The Lesson of the Cross

Rejoice in hope, endure in affliction, persevere in prayer.

Romans 12:12

At the dawn of Christianity, anyone who believed in Jesus Christ as the Son of God was a threat to the Roman Empire and its oppressive systems. The early Christians dealt with risks that many of us cannot imagine: threats, torture, public execution. When faith is dangerous, this three-step formula for Christian living makes sense: rejoice in hope, endure in affliction, persevere in prayer.

Much has changed in the Church and society since then, yet Christians are still called to take risks because of love. The COVID-19 pandemic especially taught us this. When we struggle, we tend to endure and keep praying. But what about hope? How we do foster this virtue when we're tempted to despair? The witness of the earliest Christians teaches us how hope relates to courage, for they understood the lesson of the Cross: sacrifice for the sake of others is part of who we are, and goodness is possible no matter how awful things may be.

Sr. Julia Walsh, F.S.P.A.

GOD SHINES AS THE DAY

**For you darkness itself is not dark,
and night shines as the day.** Psalm 139:12

We do the best we can to avoid those dark times that can envelop us in life. But the times come. They are unavoidable: the loss of health, the death of a child, the devastating blows of misfortune. For many people, the darkness of such pain moves them to blame God for what has befallen them. And yet for others, darkness is a time to draw as near as possible to God. They draw hope and strength from an awareness of God's presence and warmth in what otherwise would be a cold and forsaken place. Perhaps the difference between the former and the latter is a conviction that God, in the person of Jesus, knew the darkness of this life. And ever since he walked this earth, any and every dark space in life has become a source of hope, of redemption, of light. There is no place in this world that God is "not." He is everywhere as a living hope that darkness bears within itself the promise of new life.

Fr. James Stephen Behrens, O.C.S.O.

The Era of Forgiveness

"Lord, if my brother sins against me, how often must I forgive him? As many as seven times?" Jesus answered, "I say to you, not seven times but seventy-seven times."

Matthew 18:21-22

It is a very human thing to read Scripture to search for keys and answers to our own human experience. And if we were to read these Gospel verses through the lens of our own experiences, especially our struggles within relationships, the Holy Spirit will surely say something valuable to us.

For me, it is this: The era of forgiveness is not over. Contrary to the clashes and polarity we may see around us, Jesus' call to love our brothers and sisters and forgive, forgive, forgive...is not canceled.

Our communities depend on it, and our families and others in our care depend on how well we live this Christian calculus of "7 x 70" forgiveness. It may require spiritual fortitude that perhaps we've never tapped into before. We may be victims of unforgiveness before we are victorious. But the grace is there for us from the Divine Mercy, Jesus, himself. Ask him for it.

Pat Gohn

March 13

'A Steadfast Spirit'

**A clean heart create for me, O God,
and a steadfast spirit renew within me.** Psalm 51:12

WANTED: "a clean heart." Out with the old habits to make room for better ones. Our merciful God patiently waits for us to return, to be steadfast in prayer, fasting and almsgiving. We've been here before. I imagine God's restoration of my heart to be a complete transformation. Not just wiped clean—bandaged and waiting for healing. I've become comfortable harboring hurt feelings and grievances. I've grown complacent with my habitual rushing through prayers "to go get something done." The word "create" gives me hope that this clutter I've left lying around in my heart (which I've become comfortable stepping over or ignoring) is gone. Life will still be messy and time will be short. But I am different. I place my trust in God's mercy and beg to live my Lent with a steadfast spirit.

Deborah A. Meister

To Choose Love

**To do what is right and just
is more acceptable to the Lord than sacrifice.**

Proverbs 21:3

We usually think about Lent in terms of sacrifice, about what we are "giving up" in order to focus more fully on the Lord during this holy season. Some give up chocolate or coffee or wine or complaining or gossip. Yet this season is so much more than a diet from our addictive behaviors or showing restraint from our favorite things.

In addition to giving up, Lent is also a season to *give*. What can we offer, say or do to express our faith and hope in action? We can make an offering from our finances. We can make an offering of our time in acts of service. We can write letters of appreciation and send them. We can deepen our morning spiritual practices. We can spend time connecting with someone who is sick or lonely. We can buy coffee for the person next in line.

Every time we take an opportunity to choose love and act on it, we expand the presence of our loving Father.

Lord, help me take this opportunity to give, not just give something up.

Kristin Armstrong

We Are Beloved

He said in reply, "It is written: 'One does not live by bread alone, but by every word that comes forth from the mouth of God.'" Matthew 4:4

Satan has challenged Jesus to change the desert stones into bread. After fasting forty days, Jesus is certainly hungry. He replies with this passage written in Deuteronomy 8:3 about the Israelites' time in the desert. We all have desert times that test us, strain our courage, wear down our hope. We are hungry for safety and gladness and peace. Jesus' reply directs us to the nourishment of God's words. It has made a big difference for me to pay attention and copy verses of Scripture that give me life. The last words Jesus heard before he was led into the desert in Matthew's Gospel were God's saying: "This is my beloved Son in whom I am well pleased." Lent can be a listening time for Scripture passages that speak to our own hungers and deepen our trust that we are beloved.

Dear God, help me hear your words of love this Lent.

Patricia Livingston

Clearing Out the False Idols

Jesus said to him, "Rise, take up your mat, and walk." Immediately the man became well, took up his mat, and walked.

John 5:8-9

In the midst of Lent, we remember St. Patrick. It is fitting because, like all the saints, Patrick was conformed to Christ crucified in his life of sacrificial love as he, for example, returned to minister to those who had enslaved him in Ireland. Patrick did what Jesus called the crippled man in these Gospel verses to do: to rise up. At his command and filled with his grace, we can rise up from sin, suffering, fear and even death into wholeness.

It is striking that as Jesus heals a man and invites him to "rise up," we celebrate the feast of a man who composed a prayer that rings with the same refrain: "I arise today," Patrick prays in St. Patrick's Breastplate prayer, "...Christ with me, Christ before me, Christ behind me..." My Lenten devotions clear out the false hopes and idols, and clear the way for me, strengthened and filled by the love of Christ alone, to rise up and walk with him. I arise today through the strength of heaven, light of the sun, splendor of fire.

Amy Welborn

Look Within

> ...the Lord turned and looked at Peter; and Peter remembered the word of the Lord, how he had said to him, "Before the cock crows today, you will deny me three times."
>
> Luke 22:61

Peter stood back, watching as Jesus prepared to walk his last days alone. With Jesus, we step into the holiness of this "thin space," where the past, present and future merge for forty days of prayer and sacrifice. Unlike Peter who stood back, not yet seeing the glorious end of the story, we know where Jesus' suffering leads.

Lent offers us time to look within ourselves, to ask forgiveness for our past sins, to be more compassionate in the present and to place our hope in the coming God's Kingdom on earth as it is in heaven.

Jesus, look with mercy on me for those times when I have stood silently by and give me the grace to reach out compassionately with hope to those in need.

Deborah A. Meister

A POWERFUL INTERCESSOR

I have made you a light to the Gentiles. Acts 13:47

I always thought of St. Joseph as a "kindly old man." When I needed a saint, I went to the likes of Padre Pio, John Vianney or Catherine of Siena. I never thought of St. Joseph as a particularly powerful intercessor.

I was wrong. Recently, I was praying the Litany of St. Joseph and discovered that one of his titles is "terror of demons." He is noted as being effective in protecting us from evil. I started to hear stories of people's prayers to St. Joseph being answered in striking ways. Clearly, I underestimated this great saint.

It only makes sense. God chose him to protect the Son. He was married to the Mother of God. Now, he is very close to the Divine throne and has Mary's and Jesus' ear.

Have you ever asked for help from St. Joseph? If you do, you might be surprised at the graces obtained by this "kindly old man."

St. Joseph, Head of the Holy Family, pray for us!

Msgr. Stephen J. Rossetti

Heart Transplant

I will give you a new heart, and a new spirit I will put within you. Ezekiel 36:26

I've heard some fascinating stories about heart transplant recipients suddenly liking new foods or taking on personality traits that mirror their donor's.

Lent is meant to be a bit like heart surgery. It's a time to recognize that our own hearts will always be deficient on their own. Spending these forty days cutting away whatever blocks the flow of God's love, and grafting in something we lack, our hearts are more likely to function the way God intended. When they do, we shouldn't be surprised to find ourselves mirroring the personality traits of the One who gave up his heart for us on the trunk of the Cross.

Healer of Hearts, help me to understand that my heart will never function properly without you. Partner with me as I remove what hinders the flow of your love, and add in something I lack so I more closely mirror you.

Claire McGarry

Tombs and Wombs

Mary stayed outside the tomb weeping. John 20:11

Have you ever stood outside a tomb weeping? I have, mourning my father's suicide and my mother's Alzheimer's, burying starving children in the desert of Sudan, ministering to paralyzed adults living with multiple sclerosis and fighting my own battles with three unrelated cancers. Yet our faith is not only about sobbing outside a tomb of dashed hopes or a burial place of what we hold dear. No matter our suffering, we believe that Christ lovingly calls us by name in the midst of our grief. Like Mary Magdalene, we can confidently turn our face from the grave to behold Christ standing beside us. Let us go forth, in every season, announcing in our families, our workplaces and neighborhoods that "tombs *will* become wombs of new life if we surrender to faith's mystery." Then tears will give way to a summer song of joy for, in our life's garden, we have met the Lord.

Sr. Bridget Haase, O.S.U.

PATIENCE AND NEW LIFE

**Wait for the LORD with courage,
be stouthearted, and wait for the LORD.** Psalm 27:14

Life presents us with endless opportunities to practice waiting. How we wait for small inconveniences like a stoplight to change or our turn in the checkout line reveals something about ourselves. When I am able to go through the day with a sense of trust, I stop trying to control the things I cannot change. The circumstances don't change, but my attitude does, and that makes all the difference.

Recalling the passion of Jesus vividly reminds us that waiting sometimes stretches us to the limits of our faith, hope and love. Whether it is a trying personal situation or angst over the state of the world, we often come up against situations over which we have no power. In those moments, the image of Jesus on the Cross is a powerful reminder that no matter how bleak things may appear, new life can come out of what looks like a hopeless situation.

Terri Mifek

The Anchor Hold

...hold fast to the hope that lies before us. This we have as an anchor of the soul... Hebrews 6:18-19

Deep, deep down, we have a soul, the place the divine life resides in each of us. We may forget about it for long periods of time, intent on our human trappings and doings. Sometimes our soul seems to be covered up by the compost of daily living with all its concerns, distractions and temptations. Stop a moment though...and get quiet. Your soul is right there awaiting your attention.

God lives in each soul. We are kept stable on our journey by our hope in God's promises that have been fulfilled in Christ through the power of the Holy Spirit. No matter the chaos of the world, and our own wavering humanity, hope keeps us steady as an anchor holds a ship on stormy seas.

Lord, I hope in you always. Keep me anchored in you!

Jennifer Christ

FAITH AND ACCEPTANCE

Even the sparrow finds a home,
   and the swallow a nest
   in which she puts her young... Psalm 84:4

A colleague has a favorite saying when trying to figure out a puzzling or strange individual. He says, "Well, we all have to be somewhere!" It's not terribly flattering, but there's a deep truth in those words.

I often pray for guidance, asking God to put me in the right place to do his will. I ask God to give me opportunities and situations to be of use to him. Sometimes, when his response doesn't match my own sense of timing and purpose, I feel like he's not hearing me. I want God's response but on my terms.

Only that's not the way it works. Our act of faith is to accept God on his terms and learn to do his work wherever we find ourselves.

God, use me where and when you need me most.

Steve Givens

She Who Understands

Mary said... "May it be done to me according to your word."
Then the angel departed from her. Luke 1:38

Anyone struggling with the aftermath of saying "yes" following a challenging time of discernment might look to Fra Angelico's artwork, "The Annunciation of Cortona." Here the artist depicts the angel's words announcing God's plan for Mary, words that read left to right and stand upright. In painting Mary's response, the artist paints her words upside down and backward, signaling her world being upended. Perhaps even more telling in Luke's account is that after this earth-shattering news, "the angel departed from her," leaving Mary seemingly alone to ponder the full import of both the message and her response to it.

May we turn to Mary whenever we've discerned and are left to sort out the implications of our choosing. May we call on her who understands the sometimes upside-downness of life. She will surely accompany us into a graced future.

Sr. Chris Koellhoffer, I.H.M.

A Blessed Person

**Blessed is the man who trusts in the Lord,
whose hope is the Lord.** Jeremiah 17:7

I once heard that to a Hebrew, the word "blessed" meant to be
in the right place before God. I used to think that being blessed
meant having good things like family, wealth and happiness. But
apparently that is something quite different from the original sense
of the word. In the eyes of the world, one might have lost everything, hit bottom and missed that last and only train home, and
thus qualify for a place in the roster of the unblessed. Lent is a time
to reflect on God's wondrous reversals. We are asked to reassess
our priorities. I have known people who indeed lost everything
and found God in the ruins when they hit bottom. And they also
found him when they missed that proverbial last train home. A
genuinely blessed person is one whose most prized possession is
God. He will be there with you when that last train leaves.

Fr. James Stephen Behrens, O.C.S.O.

An Unstoppable Love

**Lo, I am about to create new heavens
and a new earth.** Isaiah 65:17

In Lent we are forced to stop and face the overwhelmingly magnificent message of redemption: God is doing something new! It's not that God realized he had made a mistake at first. It's not that we had botched things up so badly that God decided to scrap everything and begin again with new people.

Instead, Isaiah is painting a love that has grown so immense that it can create life, hope and a future even in the midst of mistakes, sin and death. This compassion is so divine that it straightens bent limbs, raises dead bodies and spirits, and transforms the dull and callous of heart. God will stop at nothing to make right our erring ways. He doesn't need to start over.

Yesterday I saw a brave flower poking its way up through a crack in the sidewalk. The divine Lover is like this. Nothing now can get in his way. He is unstoppable, for he has it in mind to create something new of your life and mine.

Sr. Kathryn James Hermes, F.S.P.

Raising Up to New Life

Lazarus, come out! John 11:43

The story of the raising of Lazarus is filled with high drama: Jesus' arrival, Martha's faith, Mary's grief, Jesus' tears, Jesus' prayer, the calling forth, Lazarus stumbling out of the tomb still wrapped in his shroud. Ironically, the raising of Lazarus convinces the religious authorities to put Jesus down. Permanently. The story demonstrates Jesus' humanity. He weeps over the death of his friend. "He is one of us," we say. But the story also demonstrates Jesus' power to bring dead things back to life. "He is too far beyond us," we might think. But the power that raised Lazarus 2,000 years ago is available for us today. What dead things in our life does Jesus want to raise up this Lent? Perhaps it is hope, joy, faith, compassion or a broken relationship. And there's more to this story: We share Jesus' life-giving power every time we reach out in love to someone in need. Look around. Raise someone up today.

Jesus, you who raised Lazarus and were yourself raised from the dead, keep calling me forth to new life this Lent.

Sr. Melannie Svoboda, S.N.D.

Homecoming

**Precious in the eyes of the Lord
is the death of his faithful ones.** Psalm 116:15

My earliest encounter with this psalm was as a young girl experiencing the death of my grandfather. How could such a thing be precious to God? It would be years before I had the eyes of faith to see death as a holy threshold to eternity. And it wasn't truly until my own deeper conversion to Christ that I realized that death could be a crossing over to the real life that we were baptized into—divine life in God—and how every Holy Communion and each sacrament had that aim.

Ever since we were created, the Lord of Love has been awaiting our homecoming, that we may fully experience the depths of limitless, faithful, omnipotent love.

This Lent, may we be awed by how Jesus' death and resurrection opened this door for our transformation, to enjoy union with the Trinity in heaven and a blessed reunion with those gathered there.

Lord Jesus, draw me ever closer to you. May I be among your faithful ones.

Pat Gohn

Prayer Can Overcome Confusion

Jesus then said to the Twelve, "Do you also want to leave?" Simon Peter answered him, "Master, to whom shall we go? You have the words of eternal life." John 6:67-68

Many left Jesus after he said, "unless you eat my flesh and drink my blood, you will not have life in you." Peter heard the same words and decided to stay. He was probably just as confused as the others, but he had already allowed the beauty of Jesus' life and love to captivate his heart. I think that's what gave Peter the ability to hope and trust, even when he felt confused by Jesus' words.

Life is beautiful, but it contains paradoxes that confuse us and test our faith. Sometimes we ask: Where are you, God? But like Peter, we stay because we know there's nowhere else to go. This insight comes through persistent prayer. That's how we come to know that God's personal love and guidance are always there for us, even in situations we don't understand.

Lord, keep me faithful to prayer and strengthen my faith!

Fr. Kenneth E. Grabner, C.S.C.

Strength to Love

> Be my rock of refuge,
> a stronghold to give me safety,
> for you are my rock and my fortress. Psalm 71:3

How many times have we cried out to God for protection, safety or guidance? Sometimes the world we live in or our individual situations seem so bleak that God is our only recourse, our only hope for change and salvation.

During Lent as we contemplate the passion and suffering of Jesus on earth, we remember vividly what he endured to save us. Along with his suffering came a promise for our protection and salvation. In return, Jesus did ask us for something—he called us to imitate him.

Our challenge is to look around us for those who might be crying out for guidance, for friendship, for an understanding ear. Some of them are not familiar with a loving God to whom they can take their plea. Simply put, it is up to us to show them the love Jesus modeled for us. The Holy Spirit guides us, and God protects and strengthens us to spread heavenly love on earth. The suffering of Jesus calls for nothing less.

Beth Dotson Brown

REACH OUT FOR THE LORD

Stretch out your hand. Mark 3:5

The man with the withered hand was in need of healing. Jesus could have bent down and taken his feeble hand into his own, but notice that he told the man to "stretch out his hand." Upon doing so, his withered hand was immediately restored. Many times in Scripture, we see that healing is a collaborative effort between us and Jesus, even if our part is tiny by comparison. Just like the paralytic who had to "pick up his mat and go home" or the man who yelled, "Yes, I believe! Help my unbelief!" We each have to do our part.

Our part may mean actively reaching out to Jesus or having the faith to believe in our healing or trusting him afterward that our healing is real and complete. We are reminded of Jesus' power to heal every time we go to Mass: "Lord, I am not worthy that you should come under my roof, but only say the word and I shall be healed."

Be bold. Reach out. Be healed.

Kristin Armstrong

PRAYER IN THE FLAMES

> ...deal with us in your kindness and great mercy.
> Deliver us by your wonders,
> and bring glory to your name, O Lord. Daniel 3:42-43

Hopefully, we'll never be thrust into a fiery furnace as Azariah (Abednego), Shadrach and Meshach were, but we may sometimes find ourselves in figurative hot spots. Azariah's words offer us a sample of pulling out all the stops in prayer. He reminds God of the sacred covenant and of the holy and beloved ancestors. He recalls God's promise that he and his friends are expecting to live to see descendants too many to count. He points out that they're large in their trust and their desire to follow the Holy One. And then he appeals to the unfailing kindness and unending mercy of the Divine and the fact that coming to their aid would bring glory to God's name. It's quite a powerful litany of praise and gratitude for this Lenten season and always.

Sr. Chris Koellhoffer, I.H.M.

Trusting in God

Into your hands I commend my spirit. Psalm 31:6

These powerful words of the psalmist, made all the more sacred when Jesus uttered them on the Cross, offer us profound freedom from the worries and cares that can overwhelm us. Of course, we have obligations and responsibilities that cannot be skirted merely by mouthing pious words, but having engaged our struggles and paid some price, we have to let go.

In the end, we give back to God all the work, sacrifice, joy and sorrow. At the end of the day, we do not belong to ourselves any more than we did at the beginning. These few words make a wonderful prayer at bedtime, or in the middle of the night if the cares of the day surface to tug at our hearts once again.

In the hands of God, our spirits find refreshment and renewal for what lies ahead. God knows best what we need and how best to ready us for what is coming. Though it takes some faith to pray these words from the heart, it is much harder to avoid them by putting all the burden on ourselves.

Lord Jesus, help me to pray these words in faith, trusting all things to your care.

Mark Neilsen

Longing for the Kingdom

The Kingdom of God is at hand. Mark 1:15

T.S. Eliot wrote that "April is the cruelest month." I'm no poet, but I agree that there's a certain torment to springtime. In my part of the world, after spending months of steely winter indoors, the arrival of spring is painfully gradual. When the snow finally melts away, it reveals a grimy, seemingly lifeless earth. For weeks, the land is budding but barren. Yet if we pay attention, we notice hopeful signs of spring everywhere: distant birdsong, the tinny smell of rain, the first green shoots appearing in the gray dirt.

I wonder if the Kingdom of God is a bit like that. It is *now* but *not yet*, at hand but still coming, breaking into the world but not fully realized. If we pay attention, though, we notice hopeful signs of God's Kingdom everywhere: in the Eucharist, in this holy season, in the love and care we show one another.

Lord, we long for your Kingdom!

Karla Manternach

A MODEL FOR US ALL

Peter said to him, "Master, why can't I follow you now? I will lay down my life for you." Jesus answered, "Will you lay down your life for me? Amen, amen, I say to you, the cock will not crow before you deny me three times." John 13:37-38

Peter gives us all hope. Here he was, Jesus' most ardent disciple, offering to lay down his life for his master. And yet, Jesus knew Peter was weak and flawed, every bit a human being. He would deny his association with Jesus not once, but three times. How could Peter even live with himself after this incident? But Peter is just the kind of person Jesus wanted to lead his Church. He was a man with spectacular talents as well as personal failings. And by choosing Peter, Jesus also showed his tremendous mercy and forgiveness— available to every one of us—that remain the bedrock of our faith. Lent is a hope-filled time. No matter how grievous our failures, we are promised forgiveness. We have a model in Peter.

Paul Pennick

Rousing Us to Hope

The Lord God has given me
a well-trained tongue,
That I might know how to speak to the weary
a word that will rouse them.
… The Lord God is my help… Isaiah 50:4, 7

Many of us in our human family are weary. Whether they are long-term caregivers of the sick, those working multiple jobs, those suffering chronic pain or maybe the parents of new babies who haven't slept through the night in months. People are worn out by scandals, by unending disrespectful interchanges, by escalating national and international political conflict, as well as concern for the planet. Heartbreaking human suffering is found on every continent.

We need a word that will rouse us to hope. It touched me that this passage from Isaiah depicting the "suffering servant" ends saying: "the Lord God is my help" (verse 7).

Jesus, you are the Word Made Flesh. As we walk with you this week through your death and resurrection, let new strength stir us to hope. Your tomb was empty after all that suffering! Your living Love is with us in all these challenges.

Patricia Livingston

Overcoming Deadly Events

**...the sun will be darkened,
and the moon will not give its light...** Mark 13:24

Well-wishers might tell us, "It's not the end of the world, you know," but their words ring hollow. At times, it does seem like the end of the world; sun and moon may be in place, but the chaos within us and around us creates emotional and physical stress. Wherever we look, order has given way to disaster, and the solid foundations of our world—all those people and institutions we have relied on for strength—are nothing more than fragile clay.

But the great hope of Christianity is the Paschal Mystery, that pattern of dying and rising that is a part of everyone's life. Just as Jesus rose from the dead, so we, too, can rise above those situations that are death-dealing; just as the stone was rolled back from the entrance to his tomb, so we can be liberated from our own tombs of despair and hopelessness. At the end of time, the Son of Man will return to gather his own; in our own time, he is the source of our courage and consolation, a solitary star shining in the darkness...

Shine brightly, Light of the World, in all our starless nights.

Elizabeth-Anne Stewart

BROKEN, SHATTERED AND WHOLE AGAIN

I am like a dish that is broken. Psalm 31:13

Was yours a very bad day? You lost your patience with your young children before the day had barely begun. You received a worrisome call from the doctor: more tests and an ultrasound are needed. After grocery shopping, you returned to your car and found that someone had backed into it and driven away. Psalm 31 is a prayer of distress, a cry for help. All manner of misery and affliction happens in human lives every day. No one gets to Easter without passing through some very bad days of suffering. Yet the psalmist, in the midst of dire afflictions, has not stopped trusting in the Lord. Hope doesn't mean we won't suffer; hope means Jesus came to suffer for us, to be with us in our suffering. Jesus came to teach us with his very life blood that Good Friday is not the end of the story. It seems that God allows us to be like a broken dish in order that he might lovingly gather up the pieces and make us whole again.

Jennifer Christ

A Living Sacrifice

Then Jesus said to his disciples, "Whoever wishes to come after me must deny himself, take up his cross, and follow me. For whoever wishes to save his life will lose it, but whoever loses his life for my sake will find it." Matthew 16:24-25

Self-denial. Pick up your cross. Lose your life for the sake of Christ. These are not popular ideas in our pleasure- and-power-seeking world. This countercultural message challenges my own attractions to convenience, instant gratification and results that satisfy my senses and comfort levels.

Jesus is talking to his followers here, his *disciples*. And if I call myself one, he is talking plainly to me too. This requires commitment. This involves sacrifice. It is not just a Lenten thing or a now-and-again thing. This is a real-life day-to-day thing.

St. Paul, in his letter to the Romans, captures this life with this instruction: "...offer your bodies as a living sacrifice, holy and pleasing to God, your spiritual worship" (12:1). He should know; he lived it—and died for his faith in Jesus.

Jesus, help me to willingly deny myself and pick up my cross. Send me the graces I need to make my life a living sacrifice, for love of you.

Pat Gohn

HOPE FOR THE CLUELESS

Then James and John, the sons of Zebedee, came to him and said to him, "Teacher, we want you to do for us whatever we ask of you." Mark 10:35

Most of us have a hard time relating to the iconic images of the great saints. They seem a bit otherworldly, with their eyes cast heavenward in plaster perfection. That's why, especially as I stumble through Lent, it helps me to remember the very human side of the apostles.

Just prior to this verse, Jesus has poured out his heart to his most faithful disciples. He tells them he must go to Jerusalem to be betrayed, humiliated, spit upon, tortured and executed. And somehow, the "Sons of Thunder" choose this moment to ask him a favor, to promote them above their peers.

I take comfort in the fact that these men who walked with Jesus were every bit as obstinate and obtuse as me. They give me hope that someday even I can learn to follow our Savior more faithfully.

St. James and St. John, pray for us!

Steve Pable

FINDING A SENSE OF PEACE

What are you willing to give me if I hand him over to you?

Matthew 26:15

It is easy to condemn Judas' cruel betrayal and walk away feeling smug and self-satisfied. If I do that, I can close my eyes to the times I have compromised my deepest convictions for the sake of retaining a position or have remained silent when a person or group of people were being treated unjustly. Security and social acceptance are just two of the ways I am tempted to compromise my values. In the end, however, being true to our convictions is necessary if we want to live in true freedom.

A couple of years ago, I was doing some work for an organization that was moving further and further away from its core mission to foster living in faith, hope and love. As time went on, my discomfort grew so great that I finally made the decision to resign. The price was losing work I enjoyed, but the great payoff was a deep sense of peace.

Terri Mifek

TRADING FEAR
FOR HOPE

Peace I leave with you; my peace I give to you. Not as the world gives do I give it to you. Do not let your hearts be troubled or afraid. John 14:27

This promise of Jesus' peace is our hope when we feel overwhelmed by life's problems. Life offers us many joys, but it has its problematic side too. We might have to do something that seems beyond our strength. Perhaps we're burdened by the unrealistic expectations of others. Whatever our difficulties might be, Jesus is with us to help us through them. Our trust in his presence helps us to mitigate our fear and to strengthen our hope. I don't think we can experience this strength fully without spending time with God in silent prayer. In attentive silence, we become aware of God's guiding presence within us. When we experience his presence and surrender ourselves to it, a sense of hope flows into us that begins to transform our lives. This is God's loving will for us.

Lord, increase my trust in you.

Fr. Kenneth E. Grabner, C.S.C.

Hope for Our Darkest Hours

Trust in the Lord forever!
For the Lord is an eternal Rock. Isaiah 26:4

Thomas Dorsey wrote what has been called the greatest Gospel song of all time. It is a comforting hymn many people turn to in their darkest hours. Dorsey was no stranger to the darkness and struggled for years to make sense of this world. He found music to be a language he understood. But when despair became too much for his soul, he turned to his faith. He vowed to do the Lord's work and dedicated himself to sacred music. He lifted people up in the face of their troubles—and his own.

In 1932, Dorsey's wife and baby son died in childbirth. Out of his own grief, he wrote the lyrics of "Precious Lord, Take My Hand." This labor of love became a hymn for the ages. All the credit, he knew, belonged to the Lord.

In what ways does the Lord lead you out of your darkest hours?

Through the storm, Precious Lord, lead us to your light.

Gail Goleas

Hoping for Renewal

> ...and the Lord turned and looked at Peter; and Peter remembered the word of the Lord, how he had said to him, "Before the cock crows today, you will deny me three times."
>
> Luke 22:61

We can imagine a thousand personal conversations between Jesus and Peter—their trusting love for each other and shared future plans. Peter called him master and friend, pledging his loyalty and respect. We wonder why the arrest of Jesus could have caused Peter to crumble in his loving stability. His denial to even acknowledge Jesus was the result of his blind fear and weakness; so he failed Jesus and himself. In that state of woefulness, Jesus just looked at him, and Peter returned a nervous and embarrassed glance. Their eyes must have slid past each other with perhaps a silent and voiceless nod. Any words at that moment would have been meaningless. In his heart, Peter knew he had only one alternative. He went out and wept—bitterly. What do we do when we break a trusted bond of love? Maybe it's only a voiceless nod. Then we weep and seek forgiveness and hope for our renewed friendship.

Fr. James McKarns

Treasures in Heaven

Again, I say to you, it is easier for a camel to pass through the eye of a needle than for one who is rich to enter the kingdom of God. Matthew 19:24

Our culture is one of striving: We strive for more money, more things, more status, more everything. The cliché "more is more" pretty much sums us up. We know we can't take our bank account or our things with us when we leave this world, but it doesn't stop us from trying to amass more that our children and grandchildren will have to divide, distribute or dispose of. Scripture tells us to store our treasures in heaven, not down here. Maybe we need to spend more time thinking about the kinds of collections we want, the things of true value we can enjoy for all eternity.

My mother has always encouraged us to live lives of content-ment. Instead of "more is more," she maintains "enough is enough." When we aren't clutching our things, we can embrace the real treasures. We can be rich in the ways that are pleasing to God.

Kristin Armstrong

SEE THE LIGHT

We were indeed buried with him through baptism into death, so that, just as Christ was raised from the dead by the glory of the Father, we too might live in newness of life. Romans 6:4

A few years ago, I had the most satisfying Lent of my life. Prayer came easily. I hungered for God. At the end of those forty days, I felt renewed for the work of discipleship. But at the Easter Vigil, I sat in church overwhelmed by the awareness that I was still a sinner, and the world was still a mess.

Death and darkness do not cease to exist, but instead of losing heart at this, let us cling to the promises of Christ and open our eyes to the many ways that his light shines on in the darkness. Let us allow ourselves to be joyful that love overcomes hatred, that hope follows despair, and that new life springs forth from desolation.

Lord Jesus Christ, help me trust in the promise of new life.

Karla Manternach

Touching the Risen Lord

They have taken the Lord from the tomb, and we don't know where they put him. John 20:2

In the various resurrection accounts, when the followers of Jesus discover the empty tomb, they experience shock, fear, agitation, questioning and even tears. Only after these same followers see, hear and touch the Risen Jesus do they experience amazement, joy, peace, gratitude and understanding. The contrast is significant. It reminds us that times of turmoil, pain, doubt and confusion may not mark the end of faith, but may be a necessary stage toward greater faith and understanding.

Where are you this season? Are you experiencing fear, tears or agitation? Or are you closer to peace, joy and understanding? Wherever you may be, the Risen Jesus is beside you eager to share the power of his resurrection with you. It is a power that enables us to trust, to love, to forgive or even just to hang on. Let us reach out in prayer today to touch the sacred wounds of the Risen Lord!

Risen Jesus, give me the grace I need today to trust, to love, to forgive or even just to hang on.

Sr. Melannie Svoboda, S.N.D.

Our Christian Hope

Then the kingdom of God has come upon you. Luke 11:20

I recently presided over the funeral of a young woman who died tragically. While death is always hard to accept, it is particularly difficult when a young person's life is so soon extinguished. At such moments, we search for understanding. We especially want to know that death is not the final word in her life or in ours. This Gospel verse highlights a central reality of our faith: "The kingdom of God has come upon you." In Jesus' own death and resurrection, we believe that death has been overcome and life has triumphed.

At the funeral, the sadness of all in the church was palpable, but so was their hope. Amid their tears, they had faith that this young woman was separated from them only physically and only for a time.

Each of us is touched by the painful reality of death. May we, too, not only grieve at death's losses, but also know the Christian hope of the victory of life.

Msgr. Stephen J. Rossetti

A Wellspring of Hope

Then they went away quickly from the tomb, fearful yet over-joyed... Matthew 28:8

"Fearful yet overjoyed." How could the fear of these women possibly be described? How could the joy? The utter horror of Jesus' arrest and crucifixion is now followed by an earthquake, an angelic appearance and the tomb of Jesus *empty*!

Reeling from the unimaginable reversals, they hurry to announce the news to the disciples. I think it is amazing that they could even move. Then they come upon Jesus himself. It says, they "embraced his feet" (verse 9). I think their knees just gave out from the intense tremors of the earthquake in their own hearts. He was dead, tortured, broken. Now he's here on the road—greeting them—alive again!

The Easter story is the wellspring of our most unimaginable hope, hope in God's power to bring life out of death. Hope that all our fears can be brought to joy. Jesus tells us: "Do not be afraid." Not only for our physical death, but for all the other endings, devastations and breakings. Alleluia!

Patricia Livingston

A RESURRECTION PEOPLE

If for this life only we have hoped in Christ, we are the most pitiable people of all. 1 Corinthians 15:19

Jesus taught us much about how to live in this world: Be meek and humble. Work for justice. Be merciful. Welcome the stranger. Comfort the afflicted. Suffer persecution without complaint. Many teachers from all sorts of religious and secular traditions had offered such guidance over the centuries. With Jesus, it didn't end there. He promised eternal life to those who believed and endeavored to live in a manner pleasing to God. He suffered horrific public suffering so there could be no question that he had in fact died; then he returned to his community as proof of the promise fulfilled. It made Jesus different. It makes us different. For while we attempt to live as he did in this life, we do it in joyful confidence that, like him, we will find life after death.

Lord, I look forward to the resurrection of the dead and the life of the world to come.

Melanie Rigney

Blaming the World

I have told you this so that you might have peace in me. In the world you will have trouble, but take courage, I have conquered the world. John 16:33

Do you remember comedian Flip Wilson's alter ego, "Geraldine," who consistently blamed evil for all her bad choices? "The devil made me do it!" became a common catchphrase in the 1970s. We can still laugh at the routine, but the more serious meaning behind it lingers. The world and all its evils are easy to blame for our own sins.

"The world" can be a tough place to navigate. "The world" is full of temptation and sin. "The world" is indeed trouble, ready to trip us up at every turn. But the good news and the hope of our faith in Christ is that "the world" is not our "whole world." Jesus conquered a sinful world so that we might have the freedom to live differently, redeemed and protected under God's love and grace.

Jesus, may I live in your peace.

Steve Givens

The God-Man

> ...he stood in their midst and said to them, "Peace be with you." But they were startled and terrified... Luke 24:37

After his death, the resurrected Lord Jesus appears to the apostles, but they think they are seeing a ghost. Jesus calms them and asks for some food.

Jesus was incarnated into a human body, and that same human body rose from the dead. It's no wonder the apostles are constantly confused by a God in human flesh. The God-man in a glorified body is nothing they have seen before. We, too, are constantly reconciling our expectations of what and who God should be.

Everything that we hope for in Christian life is present in the resurrected body of Christ. There is no way to understand the Scriptures except through Jesus. There is no way to love except through Jesus. And yet Jesus can be so hard to pin down, to fully explain.

We pray together that we may recognize him in the breaking of the bread.

Elizabeth Duffy

Recognizing Jesus in His Wounds

Blessed are those who have not seen and have believed.

John 20:29

"Seeing is believing," we sometimes say, but there are some things that must first be believed in order to be seen.

When the Risen Jesus appears to his disciples and Thomas is finally present, what brings Thomas to his knees in astonishment, awe and that moment of "Aha!" is actually seeing for himself the wounds of Jesus. These wounds offer Thomas irrefutable proof that this is the same Jesus who suffered, died and is now risen.

We may think that Thomas had it easy; after all, he got to touch the wounds of Jesus. But our faith tells us that even though we can't physically see Jesus today, we can still recognize him as he continues to show us his wounds. When we encounter a homeless person, listen to a neighbor's account of job uncertainty, struggle to heal fractured relationships, try to relieve a loved one's physical pain or be present to their emotional anguish, we are encountering Jesus in his wounds among us. Jesus risen, here and now.

We believe, and we see.

Sr. Chris Koellhoffer, I.H.M.

A NEVER-ENDING GIFT

But Peter got up and ran to the tomb, bent down, and saw the burial cloths alone; then he went home amazed at what had happened. Luke 24:12

Jesus foretold his resurrection to his apostles, and Peter was amazed when he saw that it actually had happened. Maybe we should be amazed, too, because what happened to Jesus will also happen to us. During Easter, we celebrate Jesus' resurrection and the promise of our own. What meaning can we find for ourselves in all of this? Easter tells us that we are so loved and so important to God that he never wants to be without us. It tells us that our relationships with our loved ones will never end. And it says that our awareness of God's beauty and our appreciation of creation's magnificence will deepen throughout eternity because we will always find more to know. Easter is the gift that never ends. That's worth some grateful thought. And if you take time to think about it, you might be amazed too! May your Easter season be full of hope!

Fr. Kenneth E. Grabner, C.S.C.

Like Every Sunrise

Behold, I make all things new. Revelation 21:5

Here's an obvious observation: the sun rises every day no matter what's happened the night before. Maybe not as obvious is that we have the opportunity in the dawning of each new day to seek forgiveness in order to begin again. We have another day to complete the work we have been called to do. Human frailty, faults and failures are no match for what God promises: to make all things new. The Easter season gives us encouragement to rejoice in the Lord's compassion, to persevere in faith and to begin every day with hope. Nothing stands in the way of God's mercy and love except our own stubbornness to resist change, to cling to our guilt or grief or anger. Right in front of our eyes, like every sunrise, God is making all things new.

Breathe in me, oh God, a spirit of hope.

Deborah A. Meister

Lilac Crush

For as the heavens are higher than the earth,
so are my ways higher than your ways,
my thoughts higher than your thoughts. Isaiah 55:9

The row of lilac trees in their full-fragrant bloom left me giddy. I loved lilacs. More importantly, I loved Teddy T. I wanted to marry him. He was quiet, kind and unassuming. His sun-bleached hair and bronzed skin were easy on the eyes. And when the nuns at our school weren't trying to wipe away his grin, his smile was contagious.

With my two friends as my accomplices and our arms ladened with fresh lilacs, we giggled and danced in the sunshine with me singing, "I'm getting married to Teddy T."

I doubt Teddy T. ever knew about my adolescent crush. And though he probably grew up to be a great guy, he wasn't the wonderful soulmate God had already chosen for me. Today, I thank God for ways and thoughts higher than mine—for those wishes and prayers seemingly unrequited. I still love lilacs. But more importantly, I love what God, himself, chooses for me.

Lord, help me always recognize that the real crush of love comes not in my plan, but in yours.

Kathleen Swartz McQuaig

May Joy Win

Then they went away quickly from the tomb, fearful yet over-joyed... Matthew 28:8

The image of these women disciples hurrying from the tomb fearful and joyful reads like an Easter antiphon in my soul. It serves as an enriching icon for my prayer, and I am the candle burning before this image. In truth, these words remind me of some of the tombs in my own life. What is a tomb but a place for the dead to rest? I, too, have experienced greeting a life I thought had died. Perhaps you also have had this experience. The hope that seemed to have shriveled up is suddenly rising again. The joy I thought had descended into Hades is miraculously visible once more. The courage that seemed to be buried in the tomb is suddenly present again, big as life, raised anew. I, too, hurry away from this tomb-turned-womb with hesitant hope and joy. My fear slowly diminishes. Courage returns.

Jesus, I spend so much of my life juggling fear and joy. May joy always win!

Sr. Macrina Wiederkehr, O.S.B.

Healing Is Possible in Christ

Peter said, "I have neither silver nor gold, but what I do have I give you: in the name of Jesus Christ the Nazorean, [rise and] walk." ...[The beggar] leaped up, stood, and walked around, and went into the temple with them, walking and jumping and praising God. Acts 3:6, 8

I love this story. It shines with what I like to think of as Easter energy. To this man, crippled from birth, carried for years to the "Beautiful Gate" of the temple to beg for alms, we hear Peter say: "In the name of Jesus Christ the Nazorean, rise and walk." And he was healed! I find the man's joyous exhilaration, practically dancing into the temple, such a source of hope. We can be paralyzed in our personal lives by resentment, regret, terrible loss. Hatred cripples our human family with endless cycles of violence across our world. This story says healing is possible in the power of Jesus Christ, the Nazorean. It is possible that we will someday walk together through the Beautiful Gate, jumping and praising God.

Patricia Livingston

Courage in Fearful Times

When they had rowed about three or four miles, they saw Jesus walking on the sea and coming near the boat, and they began to be afraid. But he said to them, "It is I. Do not be afraid." John 6:19-20

St. Catherine of Siena lived in tumultuous times. The Black Death raged in Europe, mercenary armies prowled the countryside, waging war in many regions. The Pope cowered in Avignon, France, leaving the administration of the Church in the hands of corrupt legates. In many ways, it was the worst of times.

But Catherine did not bemoan her fate. She did not say, "If only the Black Death would go away... If only the world were at peace... If only we had perfect Church leaders, then I could really live my Christian faith." No, she became a great saint by accepting her times as the context in which God was calling her to respond and live her faith. Rather than run away, she more fully engaged. We are called to do the same, knowing Jesus walks with us, saying, "It is I. Do not be afraid."

Loving God, give me the faith, courage, wisdom, spunk and compassion of St. Catherine.

Sr. Melannie Svoboda, S.N.D.

Hope's Landing Pad

**My strength and my courage is the Lord,
and he has been my savior.** Psalm 118:14

When I was a patient in a big Catholic hospital recently, my room looked out on a helicopter landing pad. At night, it sparkled with lights. When the helicopter came in, I tried to get to the window to see it. The pad was not meant to be shaped like a cross, but it looked like one. It became a symbol of hope for me every night. Years ago, when I worked as a chaplain at another hospital, I also watched the helicopter come in from the view of helping others, of having hope for my patients. Now I was watching it for myself, and my eyes filled with tears.

Symbols of hope during the Easter season are important. In Church, we look at the symbols of Easter, such as lilies, incense, the Paschal candle, the Alleluia and, of course, the reality of the Risen Life of Christ hidden in the Eucharist. In our homes, we look at symbols of hope in our crucifixes, in holy water. We look in each other's eyes too. At times, we need every symbol we can hang on to, including helicopter pads, to remind us that Christ has risen. Alleluia!

Sr. Marguerite Zralek, O.P.

UNSEEN BUT NOT UNKNOWN

Faith is the realization of what is hoped for and evidence of things not seen. Hebrews 11:1

Consider the life of St. Joseph, husband, father and worker. In the family's early years, visions showed him how to protect Mary and Joseph. Graced moments indeed. While we don't know much about the "hidden" years of Jesus, we can visualize Joseph at his carpenter's bench, teaching Jesus how to fashion wood into tables and chairs. We can see Joseph setting an example as a man who lived his faith quietly but completely, who loved God, his family and his neighbors.

Joseph didn't have a showy life; likely, few outside his community knew him. He was not the Son of God, not born without original sin. But like we are also called, he trusted in God's plan and his part in it. Joseph's example reminds us that the small, everyday things we do in hope of eternal life do not go unnoticed by God—or unappreciated by others.

St. Joseph, help me to find hope and faith in your example of a quiet life well lived.

Melanie Rigney

LIFTED UP

The LORD lifts up all who are falling
   and raises up all who are bowed down. Psalm 145:14

Maybe this spring is a time of great peace, ease, joy and abundance for you. I hope it is. We should always celebrate, enjoy and give thanks for beautiful seasons of life. But if your life does not feel this way right now, this verse is for you. Maybe you are struggling under an immense weight of illness, misfortune, loneliness, guilt, depression, loss, trauma or fear. Maybe you are experiencing a shifting season of unforeseen, uncontrollable circumstances. Or perhaps you are bearing the consequences for choices you wish you could go back and undo. Whatever your situation may be, hear the words of Psalm 145. When you are staggering under the weight of your own load, there is relief for you. Call upon the Lord. Confess your wrongdoings or your anger or your weakness and call upon his strength, his faithfulness, his mercy and his love. He will reach down and lift you up. He will redeem your life, your heart, your family or your finances. He will exchange burdens with you. He will get you through to the other side.

Kristin Armstrong

Sparks of Life and Light Everywhere

Tongues as of fire…came to rest on each one of them.

Acts 2:3

These are dark times. Everywhere we see division, anger and violence. Faith seems to be eroding. Our secular world is increasingly estranged from its Creator. Where will it all end?

But there is something else happening as well. As a university professor, I see inspiring groups of young people on our campuses on fire with the faith. In my community, the kindness and generosity of the ordinary people around me is uplifting. And I am impressed by the new crop of priestly vocations—solid young men who are strong in faith.

There is much to lament these days. But a deeper look reveals the Spirit of God very much alive and working in peoples' hearts. I suspect it was ever thus. There are disturbing signs of darkness, but these are overshadowed by sparks of life and light everywhere.

Lord, give me the eyes to see your Spirit working in our world and also in my own life.

Msgr. Stephen J. Rossetti

Answered Prayers

When I called, you answered me;
you built up strength within me. Psalm 138:3

Have your prayers been answered? Mine have. On many occasions, I have prayed for very sick friends and acquaintances. Most, thankfully, have recovered. I have prayed for people who have lost their jobs. Many have found work. Maybe it is all just a coincidence, but I count these events as answered prayers. I also know others were praying with me on these occasions and give full credit to those voices too. For most of us, prayer is all we have to offer to those in need. It is our way of "doing something" rather than just standing around feeling hopeless. More than a few of those I prayed for have no formal religion, but they always expressed their gratitude. It's always difficult to know when God is answering your prayers. Sometimes we don't know at all. But he has told us that he will always answer. That alone is something that builds "up strength within me."

Paul Pennick

Have Courage!

A woman suffering hemorrhages for twelve years came up behind him... Matthew 9:20

I love this profound miracle of the woman healed by merely touching the tassel of Jesus' cloak. It seems such an easy, quick fix. But what of the twelve years of agonizing suffering? Surely this woman, at some point (or probably several points), must have given up hope, despairing that she would never be healed. Have you or someone you love known suffering that has persisted for years and years? Perhaps it is a medical condition, a broken relationship, contentious neighbors, a demeaning boss. Whatever the cause, suffering hurts and we want it to end! The woman in this Scripture had faith, but she wanted to access Jesus' power from the sidelines, unobserved. Amazingly, Jesus senses her presence and speaks directly to her. No slipping back into the crowd now! He exhorts her to have courage and strength of heart; her faith has made the difference. Today, go directly to Jesus with your suffering. Have courage!

Jennifer Christ

Unbearable

Jesus said to his disciples: "I have much more to tell you, but you cannot bear it now." John 16:12

"Everything happens for a reason." Too often I've heard this beautiful expression of trust foisted on people in pain. Don't get me wrong; I believe in looking on the bright side. It is a great comfort to believe that God has everything in hand, no matter how bleak things seem. But terrible things do happen. When they happen to us, we don't need people to deflect our suffering with the shiny shield of optimism. We need them to sit with us in the unbearable, excruciating stew of our pain. That is what Jesus would do. Mysteriously, it is in that dark walk together that we begin to glimpse again the Divine Love we hope will one day answer all our questions. God's plan is beyond our understanding. We surrender to it together, believing that the Lord has much more to tell us one day, even if we cannot bear it now.

Lord, your ways are mysterious. Help us to trust in you.

Karla Manternach

Strength Training

They strengthened the spirits of the disciples and exhorted them to persevere in the faith, saying, "It is necessary for us to undergo many hardships to enter the Kingdom of God."

Acts 22:14

The day my mother died at home, after her five-year battle with breast cancer, we had to wait hours for the medical examiner to come to our house. He had been long delayed at another house in the city—a house where a young mother and two of her children had died in a fire. Some hardships linger for years on end. Others come suddenly.

Families worldwide lost loved ones to the coronavirus, COVID-19. We also faced numerous related hardships associated with it. Add to that our everyday challenges, and we can easily become overwhelmed.

Yet we are assured over and over again that God loves us and that we are to enjoy his incalculable blessings. Family, friends and even people we don't know will help us. We have, as the disciples did, the Church—one body to "strengthen our spirits" and help us to "persevere in the faith."

Terence Hegarty

Hope-filled Witness

**She reaches out her hands to the poor,
and extends her arms to the needy.** Proverbs 31:20

Sometimes when the daily headlines seem to scream only cata-
strophic loss, humankind's brutality and the pitting of neighbor
against neighbor, we may need an infusion of hope, a sighting of
someone like the woman described by Proverbs. In a world that
is at once beautiful and fragile and wounded and struggling, she
lives and moves among us. She is embodied in the many faithful but unnamed holy ones. They may not be celebrated for their
good works, but recognition is of no consequence to them. They
are the light bearers, those who emphatically refuse to concede to
the shadows of callousness or indifference, those whose embrace
is wide enough to gather in and welcome all who are broken or
vulnerable. Today, let us give thanks for the many who hear God's
voice and grace our world by their lives.

Sr. Chris Koellhoffer, I.H.M.

A Wing and a Prayer

Are not two sparrows sold for a small coin? Yet not one of them falls to the ground without your Father's knowledge… So do not be afraid; you are worth more than many sparrows.

Matthew 10:29, 31

A great gift for me through the years has been the way this image of God's care even for tiny sparrows has spoken to me of God's love holding me. In different times of dangerous unknowns, some winged creature has appeared. On the day before my husband was to go to the hospital for major surgery, early in the morning, I was astonished to see a snowy egret in a tree looking directly toward my window. Then that evening, right on our porch railing, I spotted a tiny bird. Just sitting there. It couldn't be, could it? Yes! It was a sparrow. I drove my husband to the hospital early the next morning feeling surrounded by God's love. The outcome of the surgery was all that we had hoped for.

Beloved God, what a gift that your creation keeps assuring us of your care.

Patricia Livingston

Tuning In

They alternated in songs of praise and thanksgiving to the
Lord, "for he is good, for his love for Israel endures forever…"

Ezra 3:11

When a long-standing rock-and-roll station went off the airwaves
in my area, a Christian rock station took its place on the radio dial.
K-LOVE promises to always be "positive and encouraging." They
even turned their pledge into a jingle. I tuned in to see if it were
true and have been hooked ever since. The keys to fulfilling their
promise are highlighting only the good happening in our country
and playing music exclusively about God. The longer I listen, the
more uplifted I feel.

God makes the same promise as that radio station, but we have
to choose to tune in. When we spend time in his Word, we're encouraged by the Good News. The longer we remain in it, the more
our soul sings of his goodness.

*God of All Goodness, keep me in your Word long enough so the Good
News fills my soul to the point of singing.*

Claire McGarry

Pain Is a Wise Advisor

Then he said to Thomas, "Put your finger here and see my hands, and bring your hand and put it into my side, and do not be unbelieving, but believe." Thomas answered and said to him, "My Lord and my God!" John 20:27-28

What makes Thomas a believer? Not seeing Jesus in divine splendor. Not hearing him preach a persuasive sermon. Not seeing him perform an incredible miracle. No; what makes Thomas a believer is simply touching the wounds of Jesus. Connecting with the suffering humanity of Jesus, his good friend, brings him to faith.

Isn't it the same for us at times? We, too, come to faith not through our strength, cleverness or achievements, but often through our pain and weakness. As someone has said, pain is a wise advisor. Often our pain brings us to our knees. Our wounds turn us into believers—especially if they are joined to the pain and wounds of Jesus, our good friend.

Wounded Jesus, may my pain and weakness lead me to greater faith and trust in you.

Sr. Melannie Svoboda, S.N.D.

LIVING IN HOPE

We do not want you to be unaware, brothers, about those who have fallen asleep, so that you may not grieve like the rest, who have no hope. 1 Thessalonians 4:13

We moved to a new city about a year ago, but some time before the actual move, I spent a couple of weeks in another part of the same town. During that first sojourn, there was a certain busy area that seemed to be a great distance away. When we would drive down there to shop, it was like a foreign place, and I couldn't imagine being a regular there at all. As it turned out, we ended up living there. It's the same place, but I'm reoriented, and now it is home.

All of us—believers or not—dwell in the same reality of life and death. But in this same landscape, we who have hope, as Paul says, think differently about the apparent sadness of death. It is the same place, but knowing that this place and all within belong to God, we are reoriented and live, not in cold grief and fear, but at home in hope.

Loving God, help me trust in your eternal love.

Amy Welborn

Wisdom While Waiting

...but the wise brought flasks of oil with their lamps. ...At midnight, there was a cry, "Behold, the bridegroom! Come out to meet him!" Matthew 25:4, 6

During a pilgrimage to Fatima years back, I spent many hours in the Blessed Sacrament chapel there. The chapel is maintained round-the-clock by religious sisters. And one sister is always kneeling before the True Presence of Jesus in the monstrance. At regular intervals, other sisters would visit to trim the wicks and refill or top off the ornate oil lamps that adorned the altar. The sisters engaged in a simple discipline of prayer and watchfulness—of keeping the lamps lit. My memory of their attentive and hope-filled witness will forever remind me of the wise virgins attending to the bridegroom in this Gospel.

This parable of the wise and foolish virgins encourages us to keep watch for him—to be ready to greet him when he comes again in glory. While we know not the hour, every heart ought to prepare for his glorious Second Coming.

Lord, may we, the Church—the Bride of Christ—be found hopeful and watchful for you.

Pat Gohn

Rise and Walk

Jesus said to him, "Rise, take up your mat, and walk."

John 5:8

We might have started this day with a sigh—feeling as if we could do more, feel more or live more. It might seem difficult to feel uplifted when we don't have what we need or when we do too much. We might sit with our feelings, weighed down and unsure of how to lean forward into life. When we begin to fall deeper into our thoughts and fears, let us stop and imagine Jesus tapping us on the shoulder, saying, "Beloved, rise and walk!" We look up and see his face; we believe and suddenly know that all is well. We rise, abandoning all that keeps us down, and we step into a new life with a hopeful heart.

Lord Jesus, please help me rise from my lowest points so I may walk into life.

Vivian Amu

Growing the Kingdom

Neither the one who plants nor the one who waters is anything, but only God, who causes the growth. 1 Corinthians 3:7

Every once in a while, I run into some young adult who walks up to me and says, "Remember me, Mr. Givens? I was in your youth group," or "You were my second-grade religion teacher!" As my eyes blink back the years and try to recall some younger version of the person standing before me, I am reminded of these words of St. Paul to the Corinthians. So very often in life we have no idea of the impact of our words and our work until many years come and go.

We are all called to plant and water the seeds of faith in those around us. Sometimes we will see that person come to embrace our shared faith. Sometimes we will never know, for the responsibility for the growth of faith lies with God alone. We are God's hands and feet in this world, but faith comes through God alone. We need to have faith in that.

God, help me grow your Kingdom, leaving the actual growth and the reaping to you.

Steve Givens

Peace Prayers

Peace I leave with you; my peace I give to you. Not as the world gives do I give it to you. Do not let your hearts be troubled or afraid. John 14:27

We rest in the presence of Jesus when we pray. Jesus does not count the minutes, doling out more or less peace accordingly. Look at the birds and flowers, he reminded us, who have no worries about how they will be fed, clothed or survive tomorrow. The world can only give us temporary peace, mere distractions from pain or perhaps fleeting happiness, which offers false hope at best. Our prayers are cherished by Jesus who promised to give us a lasting peace because he desires to be with us. A quick prayer as we rush through the day or a longer meditation on the mysteries of the Rosary both bring peace and hope to a troubled heart. Enough peace, in fact, that we can share it with others.

Dear Jesus, my deepest desire rests in the selfless love you have given to the world.

Deborah A. Meister

LOVING WITH A FAITH ON FIRE

You rejoice with an indescribable and glorious joy... 1 Peter 1:8

We rejoice in a new birth in Baptism—it continues to give us hope. If you do not remember your own Baptism, this might be a good day to go back in time. Sit on the rim of the baptismal pool. Gaze into the saving waters. You are being merged into Christ. Was that just a moment from your past? Or does this merging continue throughout your life? Salvation is a gift of God. But is salvation a process? Is this gift ongoing?

The "indescribable and glorious joy" referred to in this Scripture is a delight we can still experience. This joy comes from an active faith in Christ. It even rises out of our sufferings. Do not allow the joy of your Baptism to die. Continue to claim it as part of your spiritual inheritance. If you love with a faith that is on fire, others will be blessed by your indescribable and glorious joy.

Sr. Macrina Wiederkehr, O.S.B.

Freeing Our Grip

If you remain in my word, you will truly be my disciples, and you will know the truth, and the truth will set you free.

John 8:31-32

I recently had oral surgery to remove the remainder of a tooth that had broken off. The tooth had been a source of anxiety for some time as it had needed fillings on numerous occasions. I worried that it would break when I chewed something hard. Now that I am on the other side of surgery, I am actually relieved and happy that it is gone. It has been said that before the truth sets you free, it will make you miserable. Spiritual freedom comes only as we relax our grip on the things we fear losing. That is difficult because most of us would like to live in certainty, not faith. Hopefully, when we realize how much our fear of losing something has kept us in bondage, we can begin to let go and entrust it to the mystery we call God.

Risen Christ, help me recognize and surrender the things that keep me imprisoned.

Terri Mifek

GROWING IN WISDOM

**Then [wisdom] comes back to bring him happiness
and reveal her secrets to him.** Sirach 4:18

When I think of wisdom, I think of my mother. At 90 years of age, she has buried not only her husband but both of her sons. Instead of defeating or crippling her, sorrow and adversity have made her wiser and stronger. Like Mary, whom we honor this month, my mother is a rock others lean on. Not that she has a gift for pithy sayings or catchy phrases. Rather, her understanding heart and listening ear plus her deep love for God and her family endear her to others. She is a person Sirach speaks of in this Scripture, a person to whom wisdom has revealed her secrets.

Wisdom is often associated with age, but not all elders are wise; some younger persons are very wise. I used to pray for wisdom and then I read something that made a lot of sense to me. Pray, yes, but if you want a particular virtue, "live into it." So if I want to be wise, I practice wisdom in my everyday dealings and then one day I find I have grown into it.

Direct my actions and thoughts this day, Lord, that I may grow in your wisdom.

Sr. Charleen Hug, S.N.D.

God's Merciful Hand

For the love of God is this, that we keep his commandments.

1 John 5:3

Responding to opinion polls, the majority of Americans profess a belief in God. This is a good thing. But religious belief is empty if it does not affect the way we live our lives.

The lives of the early Christians were dramatically affected by the Lord's resurrection. The disciples lived in a Christian community; they shared their possessions; they took care of the poor; they gave witness to Jesus. Their dynamic faith changed their lives forever.

As I look over my own life, I can see ways that the Gospel has changed my life, but I can also see many ways it has not. In fact, if I compared how I currently live versus how I might live if I had no faith, I suspect the differences would be distressingly small. How would your life stack up, using the same inventory?

When we measure our lives, if we find them a bit wanting, we remember that, in the end, it is God's merciful hand that reaches out and saves us.

Msgr. Stephen J. Rossetti

Full to Overflowing

For the one whom God sent speaks the words of God. He does not ration his gift of the Spirit. John 3:34

The Easter season reminds us that we were bought with the blood of the Lamb and made worthy to be partakers in the divine nature. We have literally become repositories of the Holy Spirit, and the Spirit is not something the Father bestows in dribs and drabs. Nowhere in Scripture will you see someone only partially filled with the Holy Spirit. Simeon, Elizabeth, Peter, Samuel—they did not simply get a sprinkling. It's all or nothing when Jesus pours out his Spirit.

Knowing the Holy Spirit as a Person of the Trinity—in a dynamic and growing relationship—opens our eyes and hearts to see things with a fresh perspective. The Spirit is not just a "force," but the One who reveals the heart of the Father and helps us to love and serve like his Son, Jesus.

Am I keeping a lid on my heart, preventing myself from being awash with the Spirit's joy, hope and peace?

Steve Pable

Changing Times

Moreover, we possess the prophetic message that is altogether reliable. You will do well to be attentive to it, as to a lamp shining in a dark place, until day dawns and the morning star rises in your hearts. 2 Peter 1:19

I've been married and a mother now for almost twenty years, just long enough to recognize that no season is terminal. The tantrums don't last forever, neither does the innocence of youth. Some seasons have felt dark and long, like sitting up with a sick child waiting for their fever to break, or every minute after curfew I've waited for a teenager to come home. But I testify that people do change. I have changed. I've become more tired or worn down. I'd say that I've become more dependent, more attentive, more intermingled with the lives of the people I love. Hopefully, I reflect to others more of the mercy that I have received. Time reliably teaches us that all is not in our hands. The power to transform and renew all things and all people belongs to Christ.

Elizabeth Duffy

CHOSEN TO CONTINUE GOD'S WORK

Jesus said to them again, "Peace be with you. As the Father has with you. As the Father has me, so I send you." John 20:21

Many of the apostles had deserted Jesus out of fear during his time of suffering and death. And yet, what does Jesus say when he appears to them after his resurrection? "Peace be with you." These are words of incredible forgiveness and love. Jesus says them again and adds that he is choosing his apostles to continue his work, promising them the help of the Holy Spirit. With these words, Jesus reveals the fullness of his trust and forgiveness to his apostles, and as a result, their lives are wonderfully transformed.

The love given to the apostles is also given to us. When we make mistakes, we, too, are forgiven. We also have been chosen to continue God's work through the love and help we give to those who need us. God delights in making us partners in the spreading of his love and in giving us the Holy Spirit to guide us. Can you see how God has done this in your life?

Fr. Kenneth E. Grabner, C.S.C.

The Other Side of Pain

For this momentary light affliction is producing for us an eternal weight of glory beyond all comparison, as we look not to what is seen but to what is unseen: for what is seen is transitory, but what is unseen is eternal. 2 Corinthians 4:17-18

Sometimes our afflictions don't feel momentary or light at all. Without considering the backdrop of eternity as our timetable, our suffering in the moment often feels permanent. Without remembering to exchange burdens with the Lord, the weight of our present pain can be crushing. Many times I have been so preoccupied with the difficulty I see and feel, that I forget to look for what is unseen—God's power to transform. I love the saying, "What you focus on expands." When we focus on our suffering, misery grows. When we focus on abundance, on faith, on God's ability to heal and redeem, hope grows. We can change our vision to include the parameters of what is unseen and remember that suffering always produces something valuable on the other side of pain.

Kristin Armstrong

Ordinary Companions of Jesus

...perceiving them to be uneducated, ordinary men, the leaders, elders, and scribes were amazed, and they recognized them as the companions of Jesus. Acts 4:13

The religious leaders recognize two aspects of Peter and John. First, they were "ordinary." Would observers say the same thing about us? Would they see us as ordinary, that is, as normal, usual, real? If so, that's good. For God works through ordinary people—like the disciples—to accomplish extraordinary deeds. The leaders also recognized Peter and John as "companions of Jesus." Do we reveal that we, too, are companions of Jesus by the way we live our lives? How might we do this? By being a person of prayer, participating at Mass every week, volunteering our services? Perhaps by making choices consistent with the Gospel and by being a person of kindness, hope and joy? How might I, in an ordinary way, reveal my companionship with Jesus today?

Sr. Melannie Svoboda, S.N.D.

ACTING ON GOD'S WORD

He said to them in reply, "My mother and my brothers are those who hear the word of God and act on it." Luke 8:21

As a novelist, I'm always checking to make sure characters are *doing things* in my stories. Are they making choices and taking action or passively allowing events to unfold? Characters are supposed to be active. Disciples are too. The Lord calls us to be strivers and saints—to hear his Word and act on it. Loving our neighbors doesn't simply mean having nice feelings toward them. It means doing loving things. It means using the gifts God gives us to take actions that promote the Gospel. We are powerful advocates of justice and mercy—not because we are gods, but because we are *God's*. We use that power to protect creation; to care for the sick, hungry and homeless; to pray, forgive and comfort. We put our hope in the Lord, and he puts his hope in *us*.

Lord, help me to hear your word and act on it!

Karla Manternach

The Power of Love

If the dead are not raised, neither has Christ been raised, and if Christ has not been raised, your faith is vain.

1 Corinthians 15:16-17

I did not come to believe in Christ because I was looking for life after death. I was taught God made me, knows me and loves me and that he died and rose again so I could be with him forever in heaven.

But imagine hearing about Jesus from Paul or one of the apostles. A man—Jesus Christ—died to atone for sin. He actually rose from the dead and, by doing so, conquered sin and death. Is this true? Life after death for me and everyone I love? Sign me up.

However it is that you come to believe in Jesus Christ, the invitation to faith originates from infinite love, and our affirmative response must be from love as well. Living such love is hard but powerful. Powerful enough, even, to raise the dead to new life.

Lord, I believe in the resurrection of the body and life everlasting.

Rebecca Sande

God Delivers

For I will not dare to speak of anything except what Christ has accomplished through me... Romans 15:18

A few years ago when I was diagnosed with a rare blood disease, one of the hardest things about the whole ordeal was telling my wife and children about what I was facing. At first I just couldn't find the right words and didn't dare to say anything that I knew would make them sad and afraid.

I prayed for guidance, I prayed for the right words, and God delivered. What I ended up saying to them was that this whole experience was about so much more than words like disease and chemotherapy. It was about faith, hope and healing. It was about living a life of faith even when your back is against the wall. It was about what Christ had accomplished and would continue to accomplish through me (and them!). There was still sadness and fear, of course. But they knew that there was more coursing through my veins than chemotherapy drugs.

Lord, help me meet the difficulties in my life with the strength and grace that comes from you alone.

Steve Givens

Bringing Life

> When the Lord saw her, he was moved with pity for her and said to her, "Do not weep." He stepped forward and touched the coffin...and he said, "Young man, I tell you, arise!"
>
> Luke 7:13-14

This story of Jesus and the widow of Nain gives me a special kind of hope. In so many of the miracle stories, someone asks Jesus for help. This time, Jesus sees the woman and immediately acts with great compassion to her suffering. She has not only lost her only son, but as a widow, she has lost any protection in that patriarchal society. Jesus reaches out and brings her son to life. Sometimes we are at a dire crossroad. With the death of a loved one, a devastating rejection, a major health crisis, life as we knew it seems over. This story tells me that it isn't up to me to somehow get God's attention to help me. Jesus sees me at the gate and is tenderly moving forward to bring me some form of life.

Patricia Livingston

SUMMONING MY MEMORY

This is why you must acknowledge, and fix in your heart, that the LORD is God... Deuteronomy 4:39

When questions and doubts are storming around you, what is it that helps you to remain strong in your faith? For me, it's the strength of memory. I return to my experiences of love and beauty and remember how faithful God has been. Once I am open to it, I see it everywhere: God's love is evident in all the wonders of creation, from the tiniest heartbeat to the most distant stars. When I remember my own experiences of truth and beauty, I am reminded of what I know deep in my heart—that God is great and worthy of my focus, praise and adoration. I can love and proclaim the good news to others because I know what God has done in my own life. I can also acknowledge that this pattern of doubt, memory, return and devotion is ancient—deeply bonding me with our ancestors of faith. As they did, I can fix my heart on God and know that God's goodness deserves my hopeful, faithful response of love.

Sr. Julia Walsh, F.S.P.A.

Needing One Another

For at the moment the sound of your greeting reached my ears, the infant in my womb leaped for joy. Luke 1:44

Today is the feast of the Visitation of the Blessed Virgin Mary. The image of Mary and Elizabeth embracing seems an especially fitting one for the Church these days. No doubt these two very human women had their separate reasons to be afraid and weary as they faced the realities of pregnancy, but together they found joy and courage. At the root of this joy was the presence of Jesus, communicated by the Holy Spirit and recognized even by the baby Elizabeth was carrying. But the two expectant mothers needed each other's support to go forward in faith, hope and love.

Fear and discouragement seem to thrive when we are isolated. Togetherness certainly has its own difficulties at times, but alone, we are stuck within the limits of what we can know and see and feel. With the mutual affirmation and shared faith of the Body of Christ, our horizons widen.

Mary and Elizabeth, pray that we members of the Church might always encourage one another in joy and hope.

Mark Neilsen

Sowing Good Seed

The kingdom of heaven may be likened to a man who sowed good seed in his field. Matthew 13:24

The Scriptures are constantly exhorting us to do charitable works—reach out to help, forgive the weaknesses of others, be kind and offer encouragement. These are ways to sow good seeds in the world. It may seem these good seeds are often unappreciated and unproductive, but we must not be discouraged or discontinue our efforts.

Today's electronic society is programmed to expect instant answers and immediate results. Seeds reject this rush-hour mentality. They operate in the old-fashioned way—taking their time. They establish their roots, grow a little each day and eventually blossom into something of true value. There is no indication the seeds are going to change their pace. They teach us to be patient and to trust that if we have planted good seeds, hidden progress is already taking place.

Lord, with your help, we will sow good seeds wherever we go.

Fr. James McKarns

God Is at Work Today

When he arrived and saw the grace of God, he rejoiced and encouraged them all to remain faithful to the Lord in firmness of heart, for he was a good man, filled with the holy Spirit and faith. Acts 11:23-24

Are you or someone you know down about the Catholic Church? Do you feel discouraged when you hear news reports regarding scandals or dioceses filing for bankruptcy? Do you wish we could go back to the days before the sex-abuse crises? Barnabas has a message for us. When Barnabas arrived in Antioch, he saw the grace of God. It's that simple and that difficult. God is at work today in the Church just as it is. We can be sure of it, and we can trust what he is doing. No matter how tragic and sad the situation, Christ walks firmly and confidently in our midst to heal the wounded, to teach, to forgive, to open up new horizons. That's just God's way. Barnabas teaches us the secret of faith. By letting go of our assessment of the way things are, we make room for the act of faith. If you do this, you will see what God is doing.

Sr. Kathryn James Hermes, F.S.P.

Someday...

Do not work for food that perishes but for the food that endures for eternal life, which the Son of Man will give you.

John 6:27

We'll be satisfied—someday. We'll be satisfied when we get that big raise, except then it doesn't come—or it does, and after a few months, it feels like we're back in the same place. We'll be satisfied when the children are out of college and living on their own. Except then they stay at home, too close for comfort. Or they move so far away that we never get to see them. We'll be satisfied when the parish gets a new pastor. Except then we find his homilies boring or find that we liked his predecessor's music preferences better. Or we can set aside "someday" and be satisfied and grateful for the Lord's goodness now. We can, right now, experience the hope for eternal life that comes with faith and faith-filled works. The choice is ours.

Jesus, may I offer thanks today, and always, for the gift of your sacrifice.

Melanie Rigney

FRIENDSHIP WITH GOD

I no longer call you slaves, because a slave does not know what his master is doing. I have called you friends, because I have told you everything I have heard from my Father.

John 15:15

The French mystic and philosopher Simone Weil referred often to the "friends of God," and I have found the title comforting because there are times when I don't understand love and its requirements. I don't know how to lay down my life or how to love as God has loved me.

But I know how to trust a friend. I know how to keep in touch with a friend. I know how to consider my friend's needs like my own. Jesus, becoming man, also knew friendship, and it's here, in this relationship we associate with equality, that we encounter the Lord of all.

Elizabeth Duffy

CHANGE AND GROWTH

O, that today you would hear his voice. Psalm 95:7

The other day I went for my annual checkup and learned that despite taking medication, exercising daily and watching what I eat, my cholesterol levels are still not at an optimal level. Much to my dismay, even losing ten pounds didn't do much to improve the numbers. The doctor could see I was discouraged and said, "Don't beat yourself up. With your genetics, you are doing an awesome job." His words were music to my ears and gave me the incentive to continue doing what I can to stay healthy.

We all have places in our hearts that need to be restored to health. While taking an honest inventory of the state of our spiritual health is good and necessary, it is vital to balance our desire for transformation with patience and kindness. The voice of the Holy One encourages us to change and grow but never uses shame to bully us into perfection.

Terri Mifek

Accompaniment in Sorrow

He will wipe every tear from their eyes, and there shall be no more death or mourning, wailing or pain, for the old order has passed away. Revelation 21:4

Many years ago, toward the end of the summer, my father died. My mother seemed to adjust amazingly well to life without her longtime companion until the following spring, when her spirit crumbled, her emotions overwhelmed. As the natural world filled with greening and birdsong and buds, there was no escaping the reality that the person who had made her life come alive in a continual springtime was no longer visible. As I watched her collapse into a painful display of profound grieving, I prayed that my mother's deep faith and resilience would lead her to create a new way of living beyond her loss. Over time, it did.

How we all long for the day when death and pain will be robbed of their power! Let us stake our hope on the words of the Holy One who accompanies us in our sorrow.

Loving God, may your promise be enough for me.

Sr. Chris Koellhoffer, I.H.M.

Counting on God's Touch

**The Lord keeps faith forever,
secures justice for the oppressed,
gives food to the hungry.** Psalm 146:6-7

This consoling psalm is an inspiration for those times when life's difficulties knock at our door. When we feel lonely and weak, we can count on God's fidelity to uphold us. When we feel lost, we can trust in God's promise to guide us. When we are oppressed by our inability to love and forgive, we can believe in God's power to free us. God's love touches us at every moment. We have only to recognize it in our daily lives as we are strengthened by its power.

Lord, may my hope in you bring me peace, and may it give me the strength to become what you made me to be.

Fr. Kenneth E. Grabner, C.S.C.

Where Does Our Prayer Take Us?

How beautiful upon the mountains
are the feet of him who brings glad tidings. Isaiah 52:7

Rabbi Abraham Heschel participated in Martin Luther King Jr.'s march for civil rights in March 1965. The 54-mile march from Selma to Montgomery, Alabama, was grueling, often impeded by protestors. Afterward, Heschel wrote, "When I marched in Selma, I felt my legs were praying." Heschel's words remind us that prayer is not limited to a certain place—a church, a synagogue, a retreat center or a prayer corner. Prayer is not restricted to words or to internal movements of our heart. Prayer is not separate from the rest of our life either, but intimately bound up with what we do all day.

If prayer is genuine, Heschel implies, it will take us places. It will inspire us to do things, to get involved with critical issues of our day. In that sense then, our whole body prays—our legs, feet, hands, eyes, ears, voice, mind, heart. Pay attention this week to where your legs or feet take you. (If you're in a wheelchair, where do your wheels take you?) Are your destinations fueled in part by your prayer?

Sr. Melannie Svoboda, S.N.D.

On Open and Closed Doors

> The holy one, the true,
>> who holds the key of David,
>> who opens and no one shall close,
>> who closes and no one shall open... Revelation 3:7

How many times have we thought, "I blew it! I ruined everything." Or, "It's too late for me." Everyone can relate to the feeling of shame. As a therapist, I know that shame is one of the most painful human emotions. Hope is a powerful elixir for shame, flooding a dark emotion with light.

Once, when I was shaming myself, a wise friend said, "Honey, you can't make it and you can't break it. What is meant for you is coming to you, what isn't meant for you will miss you. Relax." And I did relax. This verse makes me feel the same way.

The doors God opens for us, no one can close. And the ones he closes, no one can open. We waste precious time and energy feeling hopeless about things we think we messed up or missed. Our God is a god of hope. He guides our path by opening and closing doors.

Lord, grant me the faith to trust your plan and the courage to proceed.

Kristin Armstrong

PUZZLING PIECES

For I know well the plans I have in mind for you…plans for your welfare and not for woe, so as to give you a future of hope. Jeremiah 29:11

I dumped the thousand-piece puzzle onto the table and stared at the mound. Disparate parts, like my then-fragmented life, dared me to fit them together. Dad's fatal car accident just weeks before, my aunt's terminal cancer and my own debilitating illness converged. I scoffed at the mound. The disconnected puzzle pieces epitomized my circumstances.

Yet as I stared at the bits, an unexplainable peace intervened. God supplanted my thoughts with a poignant message: "You cannot picture how these pieces of life fit together, but I can…" The words of Jeremiah 29:11 followed.

True to his word, God fit each piece in its place. Memories replaced grief. Intravenous antibiotics conquered illness. And puzzling elements both on my table and in my life came together. Certainly, God grew me. He fit me together in ways I couldn't have pictured. But in the process, he gave me a future full of hope.

Thank you, Lord, that even when life seems puzzling, you see a full beautiful picture with each piece in place.

Kathleen Swartz McQuaig

GOD IS NEAR

...for it is the Lord, your God, who marches with you; he will never fail you or forsake you. Deuteronomy 31:6

There were moments when I wondered if my faith was enough to get me through the toughest periods of my life. I even wondered if I believed that God wouldn't fail me.

Just when I was tired of praying, tired of being strong, I woke up one morning and the sunlight rested gently on my face. It was like a gentle kiss on my forehead from God. At that moment, it was as if God whispered, "I won't fail you...I am always near. I have never failed you."

For the first time in months, I got up feeling unafraid—hopeful and prepared to take on the day because God is right there with me. God's light of hope shines upon us every morning when we open our eyes. God has never failed us; we sometimes just forget God is near.

Merciful God, bathe us in your loving light so we may be filled with persistent hope.

Vivian Amu

Do the Right Thing

If our God, whom we serve, can save us from the white-hot furnace and from your hands, O king, may he save us! But even if he will not,...we will not serve your god... Daniel 3:17-18

Cynics say that there is no purely selfless act—that we are always motivated by the hope of a reward. We might act to garner praise or so others will think we are virtuous. We might even do it to make a point or to make others feel inferior. It's natural to hope that good deeds will be rewarded, that hard work will pay off and that our sacrifices will be worthwhile. In reality, though, we may suffer for our choices. We may be insulted, persecuted or left behind—thrown into the metaphorical fiery furnace.

Discipleship compels us to do what is right anyway, simply because it is right. God asks us to live as the people he made us to be. Therefore, we act in faith and hope, trusting in his promise that our reward will be great in heaven.

Eternal God, help me to do what is right and good!

Karla Manternach

The Path to Life

You will show me the path to life... Psalm 16:11

Most of us think of St. Anthony of Padua as head of life's "lost and found" department. This Franciscan saint finds earrings in the grass and hamsters hiding under sofas. Yet this holy man, challenged with poor health, faithfully served others. He surrendered his ardent desire to be a missionary to accept God's call to serve at home and committed himself to preaching forgiveness and reconciliation by word and deed.

Today St. Anthony offers us a spiritual road map. Lost in worries, we hold firm knowing that God finds us everywhere. Giving of ourselves, we generously serve others on good days and bad. Accepting each day as it comes, we surrender ourselves to the divine will. Radiating the Good News, we bridge gaps through understanding and peace. In so doing, thanks to Anthony's example and God's grace, we walk the path to life.

Sr. Bridget Haase, O.S.U.

More Awaits

The people were filled with expectation... Luke 3:15

That's us. We're those people still, filled with expectation there on the riverbank. When I go to Mass, that's what I sense. Even as I focus on the Lord and his presence at that moment, I can't help but glance around me from time to time, wondering and thankful. Look at all of us gathered here: so different, on journeys varied and winding, but journeys that brought each of us to this same place. But here we are, bringing with us contentment, concern, hope, despair, trust and questions. We have so much, but we know more awaits us: more love, more life, more mercy, more light. We've heard that this is the place where it just might be shining, and so here we are.

Jesus, in you, my hopes are fulfilled.

Amy Welborn

FILL-IN-THE-BLANK

> For I am convinced that neither death, nor life, nor angels, nor principalities, nor present things, nor future things, nor powers, nor height, nor depth, nor any other creature will be able to separate us from the love of God in Christ Jesus our Lord.
>
> Romans 8:38-39

My prayers of petition are often filled with a lot of strife. Yet Paul's amazing eighth chapter in the epistle to the Romans continues to keep me steady. One of my favorite confidence-building exercises is to fill-in-the-blank with whatever is ailing me or the name of the things that might be making me fearful or fretful.

I am convinced that neither death, nor life, nor _____...will be able to separate us from the love of God in Christ Jesus our Lord.

What's nagging at you? Unemployment? Sickness? Heartache? Grief? Give it a name and add it to the blank space above. Then read that new verse aloud a few times.

God always has his eye on us. Nothing that the world dishes out can separate us from his love. The problems come when we take our eyes off of Jesus!

So, try it: Go fill-in-the-blank with your fear or worry, and pray this over with Jesus.

Pat Gohn

JUNE 15

Journey to Hope

Taste and see that the Lord is good. Psalm 34:9

Finding hope in this life is a very personal journey. There is much evil in the world. Why should anyone have hope?

For me, the answer is simple. I have hope because I have come to know the incredible goodness of God. Often, I find the heartfelt cry spontaneously escaping from my lips: "God is good!" Somehow this knowledge of God's infinite goodness has become deeply entrenched in my heart. This inner awareness gives me hope and occasionally even bursts into joy.

For each person, the journey to hope will be different. God has a personalized gift of hope for each of us. If you have not yet received your gift of hope, this prayer is for you:

God of all goodness, fill my heart with your gift of hope. May your Spirit of hope not only fill my life, but may I also become a beacon of hope for others.

Msgr. Stephen J. Rossetti

ALL THINGS NEW

Behold, I make all things new. Revelation 21:5

How did an old stethoscope end up in a toy chest? I honestly don't recall. But what I do remember was its unusual role in a very real crisis. My neighbor surprised me one afternoon with a knock at the door. She was seven months pregnant. Her baby had not moved in hours. She knew about the stethoscope and asked me to listen for a heartbeat. I heard nothing. What did I know? She asked me to try again. I held my breath, trying to silence the pounding of my own heart. Still no sound. The next stop was the hospital.

Late that night, a call came in. Her baby boy was delivered by emergency C-section. He weighed only four pounds and remained in the neonatal unit for those first weeks. His eventual homecoming was filled with gratitude and joy. I discovered God does make all things new—even old stethoscopes.

Renew our lives, Lord, with your love.

Gail Goleas

Our Wake-up Calls

O faithless generation, how long will I be with you? How long will I endure you? Bring him to me. Mark 9:19

The most important things in life do not come to us immediately. We need time to open our hearts to the gifts of love, faith and hope so that they may slowly but surely lead us to a new way of living. Jesus apparently succumbed to occasional fits of exasperation when those who heard his words simply did not know what to do with them or make of them. How slow they were to experience in themselves the love he had for them—to take his words to heart. But he always countered his exasperating moments with teaching by example: praying, healing, encouraging and loving. We are called to share these same gifts with each other. We should not lose heart when we experience a wake-up call from God. It is a call that most often will come through people who love us and who see in us what we cannot see ourselves.

Fr. James Stephen Behrens, O.C.S.O.

EXPECTING THE IMPOSSIBLE

Thus says the Lord of hosts: Even if this should seem impossible in the eyes of the remnant of this people, should it in those days be impossible in my eyes also...? Zechariah 8:6

I hear in Zechariah's message a foretelling of Jesus' own words, "...for God all things are possible" (Matthew 19:26).

All of the prophets urge us to place our hope in the mystery of God's power and to trust in God's love. Our faith calls us to expect the unexpected, to never give up, because God has promised the impossible. Take for example the coming of the Messiah (as Zechariah foretold), Jesus, who rose from death after his crucifixion. Even his disciples who witnessed many miracles found Jesus' resurrection surprising. When our eyes cannot see how a situation will possibly turn out well, God always has a way to make it happen. Like the Israelites, we wait in prayerful hope. God works the impossible by changing the human heart, which only God can do. When our hearts are open to receiving God's grace, we can expect the impossible.

Deborah A. Meister

'A FIRST INSTALLMENT'

He has also put his seal upon us and given the Spirit in our hearts as a first installment. 2 Corinthians 1:22

Much of our daily life comes wrapped in legal language, in contracts and clauses. We initial each page of the mortgage, or we accept the terms of service on a website, or we squint at the fine print on our pharmaceuticals. It's easy to forget that behind all this verbiage is the trust we place in a person or product.

St. Paul goes to great lengths to prove God's faithfulness. When we hear the Good News of Jesus, we want to take it to heart, but we want a guarantee.

The Holy Spirit, the very life of God working in the world, is our "earnest money." When we see the Father's love poured out in works of mercy, in words of encouragement and even in miracles, we know that God is saying yes time and again, reinforcing loving kindness from generation to generation. God is faithful.

Lord, may your promises be fulfilled in me this day.

Steve Pable

The Wise Gardener

[The gardener] said to [the owner] in reply, "Sir, leave [the fig tree] for this year also, and I shall cultivate the ground around it and fertilize it." Luke 13:8

When I read Jesus' short parable about the barren fig tree, I say, "Sometimes I'm the fig tree, sometimes I'm the owner and sometimes I'm the gardener." I'm the fig tree when I fail to produce any good works despite my discipleship with Jesus. The owner of the tree has a right to be fed up with me and ask, "Where's your fruit?" Maybe I need some spiritual pruning and fertilizing. Other times I'm the impatient owner. I get impatient especially with people— my family, my friends, my church, my country, my world and myself. I'm ready to give up hope in all of them. Thank heavens there's the wise gardener (God), the one who is patient and knowledgeable about growing things, the one who's willing to do extra work and give the fig tree another chance. Hopefully I, too, will be patient and willing to give others a second chance and to do the work of cultivating growth and providing nourishment.

Sr. Melannie Svoboda, S.N.D.

Lessons From Job

And you shall be secure, because there is hope. Job 11:18

Job had a lot going on! Much of it was disaster and suffering. One year when I was miserable with the aches and chills of the seasonal flu, I decided to read the entire book of Job. Since I wasn't able to sleep or even to rest at all, I thought Job and I might commiserate. By the time I finished reading, my symptoms had not abated, but I was able to get some perspective on suffering.

In spite of disease, infamy, loss of prosperity and loss of his dearly beloved, Job never lost faith in God. Throughout all his pain and darkness, he held onto the hope of God's steadfast love. And in the end, his hope was rewarded, his faith triumphed, and he felt again the consolation of God's deep abiding love that seemed to have vanished, but didn't really, during his time of suffering.

Lord, I hang on in hope and faith, and rest in your deep abiding love.

Jennifer Christ

LASTING PEACE

I will make with them a covenant of peace. Ezekiel 37:26

At the Sign of Peace during Mass, we turn to one another and declare, "Peace be with you." Just before we offer a gesture of peace to our fellow congregants, the priest says a prayer that includes the line, "Look not on our sins, but on the faith of your church." How much easier it would be to build peace and get along with others if we, too, could look at our neighbors, our family, our coworkers and even strangers and see not so much their sinfulness, as their faith, their belief and their love. It takes a kind of radical transformation of perspective to establish a long-lasting peace with others and, ultimately, with ourselves. Let us pray that we can start to see the world as God does: seeing something more than our sinfulness.

David Nantais

The Light Bearers

He was a burning and shining lamp... John 5:35

On his deathbed, the poet Goethe is said to have cried out, *"Mehr licht! Mehr licht!"* "More light! More light!" Exactly what kind of light he desired is unclear, but there are many occasions in life when more light is at the heart of what we long for. We need direction, we want clarity, we look for assurance and confirmation. At such times, perhaps we've been graced to find a parent or guardian, a teacher, a mentor, a longtime cherished friend to come alongside us. Such lights are especially needed and welcome when our own flame is flickering, when the wick of our hope seems about to be snuffed out by the burdens or struggles of life. St. John the Baptist was a burning and shining light, pointing the way to Jesus. Today, may we give thanks for the presence and radiance of those who do the same in our time and place.

Sr. Chris Koellhoffer, I.H.M.

Elevating Our Perspective

...for we walk by faith, not by sight. 2 Corinthians 5:7

Thank God we don't walk by sight because our vision is so often skewed. Just like a pilot needs to trust the instruments and not fly by sight in the fog, we need to trust God.

Our human vision can be so myopic, we habitually see things only from our own limited perspective. Our fear, our ego and our perception of scarcity can inhibit us from seeing what is real or true or possible. We see shadows and illusions when our lens is cloudy. We make up stories about ourselves and other people based on old patterns and beliefs, essentially seeing what we project, not what we perceive.

When we learn to stop, ask for guidance and choose again we are able to see things through a lens of love. We can see with gentleness, forgiveness, openness and the hope of limitless possibility. God does not see things the way we do; we need him to elevate our perspective.

God, clear my vision and teach me to see with eyes of love. I want to walk by faith.

Kristin Armstrong

CLOSE AT HAND

The LORD is close to the brokenhearted. Psalm 34:19

Some of the most difficult parenting times for my wife and I were those moments when our teenaged children went through relationship breakups. We could usually see these coming, and we knew someone's heart was going to be broken. We also knew the pain would pass with time, but at the moment, all we could do was to hold them and make sure they felt loved.

With each death, each divorce, each fractured relationship, our hearts are broken open as the cost and consequence of loving and trusting. We only grieve what we love and long for, and it is precisely at these moments that we find God, as close to us as our breath. We discover God at the center of our broken hearts, never promising that it won't happen again, but reassuring us we will never be alone. In the dark, sometimes lonely days, this is exactly what we long for—God, close at hand.

Loving God, be near me when I hurt most.

Steve Givens

FAITH WITHOUT SIGNS

[Jesus] ordered them not to tell anyone. But the more he ordered them not to, the more they proclaimed it. Mark 7:36

So many of Jesus' miracles took place in very public places: the marriage feast at Cana, the loaves and fishes, the raising of Lazarus. Witnesses were everywhere; people marveled at his powers of healing. Yet here in Sidon, he takes a deaf man with a speech impediment aside and heals him. He asks the crowd not to talk about this miracle. Why does he want to keep this one quiet? Could it be that Jesus wants us to concentrate on things other than miracles?

While his powers of healing are incredible and amazing, they ought not overshadow his message of love, hope, forgiveness, mercy, compassion. When Jesus is not physically present, all that is left is belief. Our faith is more than miracles and healing. Faith is belief without signs. Faith, as Jean-Pierre de Caussade writes, "grasps the truth without seeing it."

Paul Pennick

NO COST

Without cost we have received; without cost you are to give.
Matthew 10:8

In completing an application to enter the convent, I moaned to Mama that I did not have any gifts. She reminded me that I was an excellent babysitter for my two younger brothers. Little did I know that this listing of my gifts would lead to over thirty years of teaching children.

We simply can't sell God short or think we are humble by denying our gifts. Jesus reminds us that they, freely given, are to be freely given to others. That's the heart of it. We can find so many reasons for seeking compensation or charging a fee. It takes a deep faith and hope to realize that God will supply our needs when we give from our limitations, not from any enjoyed abundance.

So, as we stroll in hope with God, let's count not just our blessings but our gifts as well.

Gracious God, teach me to acknowledge my gifts and freely give them away.

Sr. Bridget Haase, O.S.U.

The Antidote for Anxiety and Worry

Can any of you by worrying add a single moment to your life span? Why are you anxious about clothes? Matthew 6:27

Jesus' sense of humor shows through in many places, including this speech recorded by Matthew. The human capacity for worry is boundless. The suffering caused by anxiety is immense. Like the bird at the window, we bump up against our own limitations over and over and yet have trouble recognizing or acknowledging them. Our worry and anxiety grow.

We cannot help but be anxious about our safety and well-being. Of course, we cannot make ourselves invulnerable to suffering and death. Jesus knows all this—he experiences it in his own humanness, which he willingly took on. What we can do is accept the love of God who tends and cares for us and who alone is the antidote for anxiety. Trusting God won't take away our need of food and clothing. But it will answer the deepest need of all. And that changes everything.

Teach me to seek you first, my God.

Mary Marrocco

SIMPLY SERVING YOUR TIME

Just as a branch cannot bear fruit on its own unless it remains on the vine, so neither can you unless you remain in me. John 15:4

When I was trying to quit drinking, I made yet another disastrous confession. The priest focused on something I had presented as simply a consequence of the more immediate problem of the alcoholism: "I'm worried that you don't understand how serious it is that you missed Sunday Mass," he said. "That's what will give you hope." Mere physical presence at Mass means more than we might think. I've been to Mass hungover, despairing, even drunk. I don't recommend that. But it's better than staying away. Simply placing yourself in the presence of the Eucharist, even if you can't receive and have no idea when you'll be able to, is a way of abiding with Christ. Simply serve your time on your knees before the Host. Stay as close as you can. God will use every moment to draw you closer.

Eve Tushnet

Strength in Weakness

If you then, who are wicked, know how to give good gifts to your children, how much more will the Father in heaven give the Holy Spirit to those who ask him? Luke 11:13

What a wonderful promise! We don't have to face life's difficulties by ourselves. When we are confused, the Holy Spirit leads us with his guidance. When we are weak, the Holy Spirit upholds us with divine strength. These are all signs of God's compassionate presence with us. We're not in control of our lives as much as we might like to be. Things don't always turn out as we hope. We fail in some areas where we try so hard to succeed. These are painful situations that don't sit well with our egos. And yet, there is a great blessing here. If we were always successful by ourselves, we wouldn't be open to the joy of our partnership with God. It's our weakness that opens us up to God's power and love.

Thank you, Lord, for making use even of my weaknesses and failures.

Fr. Kenneth E. Grabner, C.S.C.

It's All Good

**Give me back the joy of your salvation,
and a willing spirit sustain in me.** Psalm 51:14

When I look back at the unexpected twists and turns of life through the lens of faith, I see that it was the difficult challenges I encountered that have most changed me. I laugh and cringe when I think of my arrogance and rigidity and realize how the bumps along the way have opened my heart and hopefully made me a bit more compassionate and less judgmental. While I still find it difficult to have complete trust when I am in the midst of an unforeseen event like an unexpected illness, job change or a major disappointment, it is good to remember my entire faith journey. When I do that, it helps me to recognize that everything, no matter whether I label it good or bad, has contributed to my growth.

Faithful God, lighten my heart as I ponder the wonder of your ways.

Terri Mifek

No Regrets

The Lord, your God, shall you fear, and him shall you serve; hold fast to him and swear by his name. Deuteronomy 10:20

The middle-aged woman in line ahead of me at the grocery store asked for a price check on a toy she wanted to buy. After she learned the price, she waved it forward and started to explain. It was for a goddaughter, and that wasn't all. She went on, detailing all the children who were a part of her life: nephews and nieces and friends' children.

As she counted out her money, she cheerfully remarked, "I never had any kids myself—so the Lord is obviously preparing me to do something else..."

No regrets. No sense of her path being less or limited. After all, if the Lord is present in your life, if you're serving him, listening to him and letting him lead you, do you even have time for regrets?

Loving God, you created me and you remain with me. Thank you for my life as it is.

Amy Welborn

Freedom Is a Gift From God

**All that the Lord wills he does
in heaven and on earth...** Psalm 135:6

The Fourth of July is an important holiday for the United States. Families and friends gather at backyard barbecues across the country, culminating in fireworks displays to grandly demonstrate the glory of our freedom. We are a nation that has been abundantly blessed.

As believers, we are also called to celebrate our freedom in Christ—not just on July 4, but every day. Can those who don't know the Lord see us and appreciate the joy of our freedom? Or do they see people who feel burdened by obligations and obedience? Our freedom in Christ is a gift, and our obedience springs from love and a desire to please God. Whatever he wishes he does on heaven and on earth.

When we live according to God's wishes, we are free from the weight of sin and sadness and the consequences of our wandering. Remember, it was for freedom that Christ set us free. Let our lives be fireworks displays announcing the goodness of God.

Kristin Armstrong

A Sinner's Hope

> Those who are well do not need a physician, but the sick do. I did not come to call the righteous but sinners.
>
> Mark 2:17

The great hope of a well-lived Christian life is not "heaven eventually and if we're good enough." God's promise of eternal life is not for the holy and perfect few who have their lives all together. Rather, the hope of forgiveness and life is for those who are weak and know it.

Our hope stems from a God who loves us so much that he loved us while we were still wallowing in our sins, while we lived with no sense that we even needed God. God's love always comes first. God, patiently and with unfathomable love, waits for us to turn to him and say, "I can't do this on my own."

Steve Givens

The Tree of Life

Every tree is known by its own fruit. For people do not pick figs from thornbushes, nor do they gather grapes from brambles. Luke 6:44

Trees are inspiring. Like church steeples, they lift our vision to the heavens, where we can spend some time in prayer and meditation as we ponder the hidden mysteries of life. Many years ago, I memorized Joyce Kilmer's famous poem "Trees." I especially like verse three: *A tree that looks at God all day, / And lifts her leafy arms to pray.*

Trees must have impressed Jesus for they often found their way into his parables and other discourses. He used the fig, olive, cedar and palm trees to teach people to be productive and to live together in peace. Trees show me how to endure the storms of life by bending but not breaking. Today I plan to look at trees around my home and then lift my human limbs to pray.

Fr. James McKarns

'In the Hand of the Potter'

Can I not do to you, house of Israel, as this potter has done? says the Lord. Indeed, like clay in the hand of the potter, so are you in my hand... Jeremiah 18:6

Through God's mysterious providence, humans have been given the ability to adapt and grow. We can learn to follow God more closely with faith and grace.

We can each think of changes we want in ourselves and in the world. Jeremiah's words call to mind this potential, but also that we are not the potter, which is why these hopes take shape only when we open and accept God's design.

Lord, keep me mindful of the teachable spirit you gave us from the beginning.

Julia DiSalvo

The Hope of Our Baptism

There is a baptism with which I must be baptized, and how great is my anguish until it is accomplished! Luke 12:50

It's a glorious moment when John baptizes Jesus in the Jordan River and God's pleasure with him is proclaimed for all to hear. But for Jesus, there was always another baptism moment coming—his Passion, through which freedom for each of us over death would be won. He longed for that time, to reunite the people with God.

Our own Baptisms are glorious moments too. We become members of the body of Christ, the most beautiful family that could ever be. But with that membership comes responsibility—to love God with all our hearts and souls, to live as Christlike lives as we can, to evangelize in words and actions. We live in hope and confident expectation that after our own earthly death, we will experience the true freedom the Lord obtained for us at such a cost.

Jesus, help me to live my baptismal vows authentically today.

Melanie Rigney

Remain in Me

Let what you heard from the beginning remain in you.

1 John 2:24

When I first came to faith as an adult, I could not get enough of Mass at my small parish. I have never been able to articulate just what it was that drew me there or what I experienced, but it was powerful. It lasted through decades of attendance at weekday Mass and many retreats where I was in silence for days, weeks and one entire July.

But over the years and with changes in parishes, pastors and myself, things have changed. I seek but can no longer find the fire that once drew me so strongly. Such a fading of fervor is not unusual, but it is not the end of the story. St. John tells me not to let the memory fade with the feeling or doubt the reality of my first experience of faith. What then drew me so powerfully is still there, drawing me to a deeper faith, and it is this knowledge that must remain in me.

Aileen O'Donoghue

Rejoicing Again

**Once more will he fill your mouth with laughter
and your lips with rejoicing.** Job 8:21

For awhile when the kids were young, it seemed like I was always angry. Someone always needed correction or consequences, and I forgot how just to enjoy their company. I thought I needed to present a veneer of constant vigilance and authority or I'd lose control of my environment.

A longtime friend pointed out that anger was never my default position as a child. She had been there when we were kids, and it's true, we used to get very silly and laugh in a way I never have since.

Part of the joy of childhood is trusting that we belong to someone and will be cared for. Our parents fulfill this role for us when we're young, but as adults, we still need to know that we belong to someone—otherwise we are tempted to usurp all the authority and judgment that should be left to God. Anyone would buckle under that weight.

It takes a radical readjustment of trust to believe that God will handle his own personal relationship with each of our children, just as he has with us, but it is cause for rejoicing.

Elizabeth Duffy

God With Us

I will be with you. Exodus 3:12

We all have troubles. The secret of acceptance is in the surrender and hope we bring to each trial.

I remember well my own father's death by suicide, my mother's struggle with Alzheimer's, the year of feeding starving children in Sudan's desert and my four bouts with cancer. My struggles, as yours, required deep faith that will, hopefully, carve in us more assuredly the love God has for us.

Our trials are the holy ground on which we journey to the gates of heaven. Our dependence on God is positive proof, even though we may not feel it, of our belief in the divine presence among us.

May we once again recall with certainty that God is with us in all the storms of life—not just in summer rains—and that everything is sacred. May we offer this assurance to all in their need as God did for us, through others, in ours.

Sr. Bridget Haase, O.S.U.

Hearts Open to 'Our Father'

This is how you are to pray... Matthew 6:9

With the above few words, Jesus goes on to teach his disciples the Our Father. I once read that the words of that prayer resonate so closely with the Aramaic that was spoken in the time of Jesus, they are most probably the very words that came from his mouth. They are words that encourage our utter dependence on the loving goodness of God. Most of us were taught the Our Father at a very young age, most probably by our parents. Perhaps we were taught to kneel by our bed, lower our heads and recite each word. Eventually we knew them by heart. Hopefully, as the years passed, we took the words to heart and never lost the awareness of our dependence on God. We outgrow most of our childhood. But one dimension of the heart we must keep is the truth of what we learned and prayed as children, when our hearts were especially open to God.

Fr. James Stephen Behrens, O.C.S.O.

Choosing God

**They exchanged their glory
for the image of a grass-eating bullock.** Psalm 106:20

I was speaking recently with an old friend who has left behind his faith and life within the Church. His words echoed these from the psalmist—he had left God for the "image" of a better life without the rules and obligations of religion. He felt called away from a life with our glorious God, just as once he had been called to it.

I suppose we all feel the tug once in a while to take up something new and different. We sometimes struggle with seeds of discontent that lie deep within us. But God gives us the marvelous gift of free will. We are free to choose to listen to the loud shouts and noise of the world and all its glitter. Or we can sit by the fire or kneel in a pew and hear the soft and gentle voice of our loving God calling us home. That's a choice between life and death, and I choose life.

God, help me to hear your voice in the midst of a noisy world.

Steve Givens

A Deeper Walk

Cast all your worries upon him because he cares for you.

1 Peter 5:7

A few years ago, we built a Prayer Path in the woods beside our church. The labyrinth-like pattern on the ground is a walking prayer. Journeying into the spiral, we review our cares and worries with God. Once at the center, we face the cross, the focal point of the space. There, we're invited to lay down our burdens at Jesus' feet, where they belong. Retracing the same exact steps on the journey out, we experience a lightness of being, restored hope and deeper trust.

The world may tell us to go it alone and shoulder our burdens ourselves, but we know better. We have a Mighty God who yearns to do the heavy lifting for us. When we turn it all over to him, we free ourselves up for a deeper walk into the center of hope and trust in him.

Mighty God, give me the grace I need to hand over my burdens so I'm free to walk deeper into your love for me.

Claire McGarry

FOLLOWING THE LEADER

He said to him, "Follow me." And he got up and followed him.

Matthew 9:9

Praying with Scripture, I easily imagine how I'd hopefully behave. If Jesus spoke directly to me, then of course I'd leap up and follow him! Really, though, when God asks something of me, I find I am less than eager: I drag my feet, resist and worry about my own plans. I become stubborn and selfish. I think of all the reasons why I'd rather not serve. Yet, the great invitation of today, of this time, is to make service to God a priority. When we do, we can't help but become different. As we serve, we'll realize that we won't just be influencing others. We will also find ourselves changing for the better. Through each act of selfless love, our minds and hearts are joined more closely to Christ.

Jesus, give me the courage to follow you and let you change my life.

Sr. Julia Walsh, F.S.P.A.

NOT IN VAIN

Though I thought I had toiled in vain,
  and for nothing, uselessly, spent my strength,
Yet my reward is with the Lord... Isaiah 49:4

I poured hours of hard work into my presentation for the meeting. I was told I had thirty minutes, but we started late and I only had fifteen. I fumbled quickly through my presentation slides and was unable to fully develop my initiative. The preoccupied and distracted looks of my colleagues signaled the flat reception of my ideas. Rather than the enthusiasm, and perhaps even applause, I had hoped for, they were all checking their phones and shuffling their papers. I left the meeting dejected and feeling I had toiled in vain. Yet, deep down, I do believe the Lord appreciates my efforts. They are not wasted. Somehow, God is using this experience for a greater good. I gained knowledge and practiced many new skills in my preparation. I gave my best! I faced disappointment, yet hope against hope, I may have planted some seeds for future germination. God uses everything in his unfolding plan. I trust and persevere.

Jennifer Christ

What Love Really Is

Love is patient, love is kind. 1 Corinthians 13:4

This passage from First Corinthians, so popular as a reading for weddings, can easily be passed over as just another sentimental expression of the word "love." But when read slowly and thoughtfully, St. Paul's description of what love is and is not reveals a harder edge than most contemporary uses of the word. The kind of love Paul describes is not easy to come by, much less display day in and day out. Like its partners of faith and hope, love must be renewed in us continually, not by force of will or fervent study or bold actions, but by the grace of God. Paul wants us to see what love really is, not so we can grasp and possess it, but so that we can recognize, strive after and appreciate it when it shows up in our lives.

Lord Jesus, help me to love as you love us all.

Mark Neilsen

'Test Everything'

Test everything; retain what is good. 1 Thessalonians 5:21

This tiny passage has always been a favorite of mine. Too often, I've heard believers accused of "blind faith" because we trust in what we cannot see. Yet we do not believe without evidence. We are informed by the testimony of others, passed down and protected by the Holy Spirit through generations. We draw upon our own experiences too: the love we have known, the goodness we have tasted, our own relationship with the Lord.

Our task as believers is to test everything in the light of the Gospel message—to ask questions with humility and openness. God gave us reason so that we might draw near to him and know him better. Reason allows us to ponder the intricacy of his designs—with the naked eye, under the microscope and through telescopes pointed at the sky. The Truth can withstand such scrutiny. Faith is not blind. It is clear-eyed and full of hope.

Lord, help me to see with the eyes of faith!

Karla Manternach

Accepting Where God Takes Us

Amen, I say to you, whoever does not accept the kingdom of God like a child will not enter it. Mark 10:15

Once, long ago, life was getting to me, so I buckled my toddler daughter in the car, and we took off for the beach. I didn't even make clear to her where we were going. We just went.

We arrived, and she played, delighted as I sat and pondered. All this time, she had never questioned where we were going, never fought it. She had just come along for the ride, accepting and happy.

I could have seen naïveté in her acceptance, and perhaps that is one way to look at it. But at the time, I simply saw trust—trust in where I was taking her because she trusted that I loved her and would only want the best for her.

Like God's love for me, can I accept where he takes me?

Lord, I trust you and welcome your reign of love in my life.

Amy Welborn

JESUS, OUR LIGHT IN DARKNESS

I came into the world as light, so that everyone who believes in me might not remain in darkness. John 12:46

A friend recently showed me a precious family heirloom: her uncle's miner's lamp. It was from the age before such lamps were powered by batteries. Her uncle's lamp was a small gray metal lantern—about 5 inches high—with a hook on it to secure it to his miner's hat. A gauge on the lamp warned the miner when the fuel was getting low. How important it was to have such a gauge! No one would want to be caught without light in the total darkness of a coal mine.

In a way, we can say that Jesus is our "miner's lamp." He illumines our way as we negotiate the darkness of human living. What darkness? Ill health, the death of a loved one, the loss of a job, the worry over a child or grandchild, the fear of violence, the ache of loneliness, ignorance, a difficult decision that must be made. How important it is to check the gauge regularly to be sure we have sufficient fuel to keep our light shining.

Jesus, you are the light of my life. Direct all my steps today.

Sr. Melannie Svoboda, S.N.D.

SUFFERING MISUNDERSTOOD

Christ suffered for sins once…that he might lead you to God.

1 Peter 3:18

People often talk about suffering as something to endure. They may even add that it can be meritorious. This is true, but I think it misses the depths.

When a child is sick, loving parents will sacrifice their own night's rest, even exposing themselves to the illness, to nurse the child. They will likely say they want to be with the child, not as a burden, but out of love. Similarly, Jesus, despite a natural human aversion to suffering, willingly embraced the Cross. He did so out of love for us, his spiritually sick children.

There are many crosses in every life. If we embrace them out of love of God and neighbor, we will be united to the infinite love of Jesus' Cross. Then, the "burden will be light" (Matthew 11:30), and it will be a source of grace for others and for ourselves.

Msgr. Stephen J. Rossetti

Be Coachable

Your ways, O Lord, make known to me;
   teach me your paths.
Guide me in your truth and teach me,
   for you are God my savior... Psalm 25:4-5

All mentors, spiritual directors or managers providing specialty training long for their protégés to attend to their learning with a teachable spirit. Similarly, the hardest-working athletes and artists and astronauts are often found to be the most coachable, the most willing to learn their sport, craft or scientific endeavor from the ground up from a master within their field.

The spiritual life is no different.

The psalmist here pleads to be taught and guided by the Lord himself. This is a humble posture, one that reveres and respects God. But it also a posture of familiarity and one rich in hope, for the humble learner recognizes the kindness and goodness of the Lord.

How about us—are we willing to be taught? (We are never too old for this.) How can we become more receptive to the Lord's coaching of us? How can we be better attuned to God's will for us?

Pat Gohn

THE GOOD SHEPHERD

I am the good shepherd, and I know mine and mine know me… I will lay down my life for the sheep. John 10:14-15

As a child, the first piece of Scripture I ever memorized was Psalm 23. Those first five words, "The Lord is my shepherd," are so ingrained in my memory that I cannot imagine *not* knowing them. Growing up a city kid, I didn't have many opportunities to see either sheep or shepherds, but I have known for a long time that I had a relationship with Christ like that of a sheep to its shepherd.

Within that relationship resides the beauty of our faith. For our faith is not blind, nor is it a childish and irrational belief in something that cannot be seen. Our faith is alive and as real as a shepherd sitting on an ancient hillside, his hand on the napes of our necks and his eyes never resting as he scans the flock in search of danger. Our faith is about this kind and ever-loving shepherd who has claimed us for his own, knows us by name and has, in fact, already sacrificed his life for our own.

Lord, be my shepherd and my guide.

Steve Givens

We Don't Know God's Plans

Why did Sarah laugh… Is anything too marvelous for the Lord to do? Genesis 18:13-14

We fear strangers and may lock the doors to keep them out, but our ancestors could not have survived in the desert without hospitality. Abraham ran down the road to welcome the three men. Sarah stayed in the tent and prepared the meal.

Strangers were often curious. *Where are your children?* they wonder. Sarah kept her sadness hidden as she stuck to her tasks. This was not the life she had anticipated. But Sarah laughed to herself: This stranger's promise of a child to come made no sense, given her age.

Sarah was sure that no one was listening. But God had other plans. Our persistent longings are heard somehow. There is more joy in store than we can imagine. Abraham and Sarah's son, Isaac, indeed would be "the laughter of God."

God, help us to believe that our lives can bear fruit.

Jeanne Schuler

A LIFELONG SOURCE OF HELP

You are my hope, LORD;
  my trust, O God, from my youth.
On you I depend from birth;
  from my mother's womb you are my strength;
  constant has been my hope in you. Psalm 71:5-6

My Bible labels Psalm 71 "a prayer in time of old age." Recently we buried one of our oldest parishioners. Jack was a 97-year-old veteran of World War II. He joined the Army Air Corps at 17, as an ROTC graduate who happened to have a pilot's license. Soon he was flying B-17s and B-52s from the U.S. to London to prepare them for action in Europe.

Not all of us will have a life story as dramatic as Jack's, but the Lord is our constant source of hope, stability and protection. From the womb to the tomb, the God of Israel—the very Lord of the cosmos—sustains us with infinite compassion and faithfulness. Whether we are in a cockpit or foxhole, or anxious at a loved one's bedside, or looking for work, or fretting over finances, Jesus is there to bring light and refuge.

Steve Pable

What a Story!

Then beginning with Moses and all the prophets, he interpreted to them what referred to him in all the scriptures.

Luke 24:27

The disciples on the road to Emmaus—what a story! We can just imagine ourselves asking the anguished, utterly ironic question: "Are you the only visitor to Jerusalem who does not know of the things that have taken place there in these days?" (Luke 24:18). Terrible things had taken place—the crucifixion and death of Jesus—ripping apart their hopes and their hearts.

It has always fascinated me that Jesus responded by showing them the Scriptures "beginning with Moses and all the prophets." I wonder what he said that had their hearts burning on the road. Along with the figure of the suffering Messiah, did he point out how God brought amazing life out of hopeless situations? The Red Sea parting, the whale unswallowing Jonah, the field of dry bones becoming living, breathing people?

Each time we are faced with some terrible thing, we need the stories of the Love that saves us, the Love that walks right beside us on the road.

Patricia Livingston

Singing a New Song

Sing to the Lord a new song... Psalm 98:1

Perhaps we're counted among them at this moment, the many in our world struggling to sing a new song. In that choir is the person longing to overcome addictive behavior; the mother caught in an abusive relationship that threatens her life and the safety of her children; the widow, widower, orphan who can do nothing but weep over the loss of a loved one; the immigrant or refugee displaced from all that sings of home and the familiar.

When our pain is so profound that the words catch in our throat, when terror, despair, numbness cause us to lose the melody, our faith assures us that even then, God continues to sing in us.

What is the new song that God is calling us to enter into today?

Sr. Chris Koellhoffer, I.H.M.

Soften the Soil

**And some seed fell on good soil, and when it grew, it pro-
duced fruit a hundredfold.** Luke 8:8

God's Word can be disruptive. Just like tree roots buckle sidewalks
as they grow, the Word of God can challenge and change us. It
prompts us to challenge and change our fallen world as well. It
only does that, however, if we allow it to take root in our hearts.
Do we? Are we rich soil or shaky ground? The truth is, we are not
only one or the other. Sometimes we open our hearts and respond
to what God seems to ask of us. Sometimes we deflect God's Word
and refuse to answer its call.

What are we doing right now? Can we take this time in prayer
to soften the soil of our hearts and ask God to entrust his Word to
us?

Lord God, plant your Word within me to produce a hundredfold!

Karla Manternach

Hope Behind Bars

When he entered Rome, Paul was allowed to live by himself, with the soldier who was guarding him. Acts 28:16

I am amazed at the number of times St. Paul was arrested and placed in prison, as described in the Acts of the Apostles and in his epistles. His incarcerations were for violations of Jewish and Roman religious laws. Some of these were overnight or a few days, and others were as long as two years. It is estimated that Paul was in prison at least a total of six years.

I recently read that in the United States, there are close to two million people in prison. Whatever the crime may be or the degree of guilt one may have, perhaps St. Paul could be a patron of hope for prisoners. He used his prison time for prayer and conversation about faith and trust in God. He wrote some of his most impressive letters during his two years in the Roman prison. His body was confined by bars or walls, but not his spirit.

Lord, wherever we are, help us, as you did Paul, to find hope in tomorrow.

Fr. James McKarns

From Misery to Renewal

**A clean heart create for me, O God,
and a steadfast spirit renew within me.** Psalm 51:12

I love how this psalm is called the *Miserere*: Prayer of Repentance. David wrote this after Nathan the prophet came to admonish him for his affair with Bathsheba. Anyone who has ever royally screwed up can relate to the word *miserere*, which conjures up the word misery, because this is exactly how sin feels. Psalm 51 is the place I go when my heart is heavy and I am in need of confession. David puts into words how we all feel, and there is some comfort in knowing that even this great king, this beloved man of God, was also a royal screwup. This prayer of repentance shows David's humility and remorse, but also his absolute belief that God can and will redeem him. He knows his only hope to start over is in God's hands. Hopefully we all have Nathans in our lives, the people who call us out and call us higher. And hopefully we learn to plunge ourselves fully into repentance, calling on God for clean hearts and steadfast spirits.

Kristin Armstrong

Steps to Glory

...do everything for the glory of God. 1 Corinthians 10:31

This is a very familiar phrase for many people. St. Paul wrote it and lived it. St. Ignatius of Loyola later popularized its message, with his famous motto that undergirded the founding of the Jesuit order: "For the greater glory of God." (In Latin, *Ad Maiorem Dei Gloriam*, or *A.M.D.G.* for short.)

But *how* to live this way? This is a call to be all in for God. It's a radical commitment to a living faith. To root out sin and vice and be converted. To admit we don't have all the answers and to strive to accept the truth of the Gospel. To act with the end—God's glory—in mind. To ask the tough questions of myself—will what I'm doing this day, *this hour,* bring glory of God? And, if not, am I willing to change course?

I'd be lying if I said I've got this figured out. But I'm willing to take more deliberate steps toward glory. What gives me great hope is that both of these great saints—Paul and Ignatius—started out with the same raw materials that you and I have. We all get one life to live. We're all invited to make some glory-bound choices. What are we going to do with our hope-filled choices?

Pat Gohn

Life Prayer

And whatever you do, in word or in deed, do everything in the name of the Lord Jesus, giving thanks to God the Father through him. Colossians 3:17

One day as a young mom, I lamented to a religious sister that I'd fallen asleep trying to pray. She laughed good naturedly, "Honey, right now *your life* is a prayer!" What a gift that woman gave me. Her words still inspire hope in me.

It's not that I didn't pray prior to sister's sage encouragement, but that I relegated prayer to separate events. Daily Mass and Adoration were special set-apart times—as they should be. But I lacked the integration of *life* as prayer.

When I learned to share completely with God—to thank him for parking places and beautiful sunsets, to pray amid a child's frustration or intercede for someone's immediate need—it changed me for the good. It transformed my prayer life to a life-prayer.

Inviting God into the midst of my sometimes-messy daily life means we're together in everything. And that's a prayer worth living.

O Lord, whether I'm alert and oriented, or sleeping soundly, may I continually live my life as a prayer to you.

Kathleen Swartz McQuaig

The Challenge to Trust

Trust in him at all times, O my people! Psalm 62:9

When I was a boy, a friend had a tree house in his backyard. I spent a summer trying to get the courage to climb the rickety ladder and hoist myself onto its platform. I would always look down and grow afraid of how high up I was.

As I grow older, I find that trust in the Lord is often my biggest challenge. I am too aware of the risks and the pitfalls, whether it be health or wealth, whether it be changes in my profession or changes in the lives of my children. With age, trusting in the Lord becomes more necessary and yet seemingly more difficult.

I think the Psalms were written for those of us who are older. God is my rock, the psalmist sings, encouraging us to pour out our hearts to the Lord, even when our trust wavers. He assures us that only "in God is my safety and my glory" (verse 8).

Holy Spirit, grant me the courage to trust steadfastly in the goodness of the Lord.

Greg Erlandson

Follow the Leader

Then he said to all, "If anyone wishes to come after me, he must deny himself and take up his cross daily and follow me."

Luke 9:23

Quick, what's your cross?

Maybe your cross is a parent who doesn't appreciate all the caregiving and emotional and financial support you try to provide. Maybe your cross is a child or spouse engaged in destructive, addictive behaviors. Maybe your cross is a fondness for gossip or negativity or worry.

Crosses. They're all different, and we all have them. They seem almost unbearable to carry, and it's tempting instead to indulge in pity parties about how cruel the world is. But rather than lie down and surrender to our crosses' weight and splinters, Jesus calls us to do what he did each and every day of his life on earth, never more visibly and painfully than on the way to his crucifixion: pick up that cross and follow. He's there every step of the way, offering to shoulder part of the burden—if we're willing to invite his aid.

Jesus, my weight and heart are heavy. Please help me take up my cross.

Melanie Rigney

Our Prayers Are Heard

He who honors his father is gladdened by children,
    and when he prays he is heard.
He who reveres his father will live a long life;
    he obeys the Lord who brings comfort to his mother.

Sirach 3:5-6

When my mother first began to show signs of Alzheimer's disease, I remember one specific phone call. After a few minutes she suddenly said, "Who is this?" I told her and she apologized just as quickly. "Oh, I'm just forgetting so much lately." During the same call she could not remember my birthday. Our family all hoped Mom was just having "senior moments." Instead it was the beginning of a fundamental shift as children became caregivers for a parent.

Seeing loved ones in failing health can exact an emotional toll. There is sorrow, of course, but anger too—at doctors who can't cure, at loved ones for not healing, at God for not intervening. Overcoming the roiling emotions means going deep within for the patience, compassion, kindness and consideration that will be needed as we assume the duties of caretaker. The grace will be given. Our prayers will be heard.

Paul Pennick

August 4

Faith Is Our Life

> During the night, the angel of the Lord opened the doors of the prison, led them out, and said, "Go and take your place in the temple area, and tell the people everything about this life." Acts 5:19-20

As I prepared this devotion, I was struck by the words, "tell the people everything about this life." The phrase "this life" underscored for me that, for the early Christians, faith in Jesus was not a pastime, diversion or sport. It was their life. It was a commitment of their whole selves to the person and teachings of Jesus. As such, their faith formed their attitudes. It shaped their decision-making. It determined their choices. Sometimes their faith led them to prison or even to death in the public arena.

What about my faith? Is it a pastime, or is it central to my life? Is it a mere interest I have, or does it lie at the heart of who I am and all I do?

Jesus, may you and your teachings be at the core of who I am and all I do.

Sr. Melannie Svoboda, S.N.D.

Underdogs of Hope

> Be utterly amazed!
> For a work is being done in your days
> that you would not believe, were it told. Habakkuk 1:5

In 1975, Sylvester Stallone watched Chuck Wepner, a liquor salesman from New Jersey, knock down the heavyweight boxing champion Muhammad Ali. It inspired Stallone to take his failing acting career in a new direction. He wrote the script for *Rocky* in three nights. With just $106 in the bank, he refused to sell the script until the producers agreed to cast him as the lead. The hope Wepner inspired in Stallone led to nine Oscar nominations, three wins and $200 million in gross sales.

God is always placing underdogs of hope all around us. Often, they're the people and circumstances we least expect. When we remain open and willing, God uses them to inspire us to go in new directions, ones that always lead to new life.

God of Surprises, open my eyes to the wonders you place in my path to inspire me to new life.

Claire McGarry

The Holy Act of Waiting

Since the bridegroom was long delayed, they all became drowsy and fell asleep. Matthew 25:5

We seek to be intimately united with Christ, but the consolations and fervor of our Christian vocation can come and go. Sometimes we may feel the lack of God's presence and wonder why, in spite of God's love for us, we still feel tired, alone, hungry or longing.

We should not condemn this feeling of lack. It is the source of our desire for God. Wisdom is knowing that nothing but God can fulfill it. We may get bored with waiting. We want to busy ourselves with work, devotions, relationships or consumption of food and material goods. But even now in summer, as the Advent seasons of the past have taught us, waiting is itself a holy act. Waiting acknowledges that we are powerless to save ourselves.

Lord, help me to trust that you will arrive!

Elizabeth Duffy

Everything I've Done Today

> At dawn let me hear of your kindness,
>   for in you I trust.
> Show me the way in which I should walk,
>   for to you I lift up my soul. Psalm 143:8

If you're familiar with Alfred Hitchcock's movies, you know that they often center on an ordinary person caught up in shenanigans. People going about their business stumble upon events and end up not only saving their own skin, but righting a greater wrong in the process. I think it's an appealing scenario because it reflects, albeit in more extreme terms, much of what we experience every day. We walk out the door, and right away, we're plunged into life—our actions matter, our interactions have an impact: in the grocery store line, in that work meeting, with family, friends and strangers. I hopefully won't end the day running from airplanes or hanging from a cliff, but everything I've done today will indeed have an impact—letting Jesus love through me, I'll do my best to make sure it's for the good.

Amy Welborn

Facing Obstacles

...the Lᴏʀᴅ swept the sea with a strong east wind throughout the night and so turned it into dry land. Exodus 14:21

When we fall in love with God, we can have delightful moments of just wanting to go wherever God goes. At other moments, though, going with God is less lovely. Obstacles appear along the path. Things get frightening and discouraging. We wonder, "Have I gone the wrong way? Has God misled me?" It's agonizingly difficult not to give up or turn back.

But sometimes we find the courage and faith to meet that obstacle and not run away, especially if others help us. How else could the Israelites have met the immeasurable obstacle of the great Red Sea, stopping them perilously in their flight from the furious pursuing armies of Pharaoh? They had the leadership of Moses, the encouragement of one another, their many years' spiritual training and the Word of God to sustain them. The obstacle became a doorway.

Lord, help us keep faith in the face of insurmountable obstacles until you open the path for us.

Mary Marrocco

True to His Promise

And, behold, I am with you always, until the end of the age.

Matthew 28: 20

Often family gatherings become "Remember when?" celebrations. Last moments and last words from our beloved departed are relished and shared. Jesus is our Brother, so we are family. His last words before ascending to his Father are treasures of hope and possibility. The Son of God, our God-made-flesh—a man of his Word—promises to never leave us.

When life is a challenge or we face a cliff of despair, let us hold fast to the promise of our Brother, and may we continue our journey hand in hand with him. We need the faith to believe, the patience to wait and his light to hope.

No Cross, no Crown...plain and simple. Yet we have a divine promise to cling to and a Brother who loves us beyond measure, both pledges of infinite hope.

Jesus, may your promise to be with me always bring me deep and lasting hope.

Sr. Bridget Haase, O.S.U.

DAILY ARMOR

But since we are of the day, let us be sober, putting on the breastplate of faith and love and the helmet that is hope for salvation. 1 Thessalonians 5:8

To combat the coronavirus pandemic, we had to get used to "masking up" every time we went out in public or met with people outside our "bubble." We had to put on our protection against the virus known as COVID-19. We tucked extra masks in our pockets, purses and cars. For some, their masks became fashion statements, color-coordinating with their outfits.

In this verse from 1 Thessalonians, Paul urges us to suit up with a different type of protection: the armor of faith, love and hope. He acknowledges the challenges of our human life: we are *of the day*, whatever it holds. We must take our lives seriously: *be sober*.

Today, suit up with eternal protection: faith, love and hope. Don't leave the house without it!

Oh Lord, as I put on the helmet of hope, I open my day to your plan.

Jennifer Christ

'He Is Not Far'

> ...so that people might seek God, even perhaps grope for him and find him, though indeed he is not far from any one of us.
>
> Acts 17:27

Many years ago as a member of a young adult faith group, I went on my first and only spelunking adventure in an ancient cave beneath the Ozark hills of southern Missouri. I remember that at one point we all turned off our flashlights and experienced total, utter darkness. I literally could not see my hand in front of my face, and for a terrifying moment, I imagined what it would be like to have to grope my way out of the cave, inch by inch, not knowing if I would ever see the light of day again.

In our journeys of faith, we sometimes experience "dark nights of the soul" when God seems nowhere to be found, and darkness masks any sense of light, hope or joy. But the mystery and majesty of our relationship with Christ is that he is, in fact, always near, standing close by and awaiting our reaching hands to stretch out to him in prayer, yearning for his touch.

Jesus, see me in the darkness. Show me your light.

Steve Givens

COMMUNITY OF FAITH

So the other disciples said to [Thomas], "We have seen the Lord." But [Thomas] said to them, "Unless I see the mark of the nails in his hands and put my finger into the nail marks and put my hand into his side, I will not believe." John 20:25

As I nursed my doubts about faith and fought the urge to skip Mass, I thought about this Gospel passage. We are told that Thomas is late showing up. His friends, maybe even some of his family, greet him with an astonishing story. I know the feeling Thomas must have had at that moment, wondering if these friends were just teasing him because he's late to the party, again. Thomas asks for proof of Jesus' return. Physical proof. He probably hears this incredible story a few times from his friends, encouraging Thomas to hang around with them. A week later, in the presence of these friends and family, Thomas experiences the Risen Christ.

When I separate myself from the community of believers, my faith falters. The presence of Christ is felt in the Eucharist at Mass and physically in the love of family and friends who strengthen my faith.

Deborah A. Meister

God Accepts Us Unconditionally

**The LORD lifts up all who are falling
and raises up all who are bowed down.** Psalm 145:14

These words express two of the deepest needs of the human heart. When we make mistakes, we long for the forgiveness of God who loves us unconditionally. And when life's challenges wear us down, we long for the divine help that raises us up. The good news is that divine forgiveness and help are ours for the asking. This promise runs like a thread throughout sacred Scripture, and it is the primary source of our courage and joy.

We will never be fully free from faults in this life, and we certainly will never be in full control of our lives, but that's OK. We can't escape the human condition. The good news is that God accepts us as we are, loving us in our successes as well as in our failures. What a tremendous reason for joy!

Lord, your love is my support. May I always trust in you. And may I imitate you by being a support to others in their needs.

Fr. Kenneth E. Grabner, C.S.C.

OUR MOTHER'S BEAUTIFUL FACE

Most blessed are you among women... Luke 1:42

My first thought on this feast of the Assumption of the Blessed Virgin Mary is that of my mother. In her sixties, she walked down to the rectory, knocked on the door and said to the pastor that she wanted to become Catholic. Several months later, on the feast of the Assumption, she entered the Church. Like many converts, she became an exemplary Catholic, which included serving as an extraordinary minister of the Eucharist, a task she loved. Each year, she celebrated this feast with a special gratitude and joy.

Not long ago, she passed on. And I am confident that the Blessed Mother welcomed her into the Kingdom. There are many beautiful gifts in our Catholic faith. We especially love Jesus in the Eucharist, and we love to look upon the beautiful face of our Mother. These give me great joy, and they did so for my mother as well. How about for you?

Msgr. Stephen J. Rossetti

RISING UP, MOVING ON

Rise, pick up your stretcher, and go home. Matthew 9:6

Speaking to a paralyzed man, Jesus is using the situation to illustrate to the scribes that he holds the power to forgive sins—which is just as dramatic a recovery for the human condition as a paralyzed man standing up and walking. Whether we are crippled by sin or by the frail state of our bodies, a key component of recovery is that we must rise. We have to have enough faith to stand up and walk out our healing. How would the paralyzed man know he had been healed if he never stood up and tried to walk?

The same goes for us. If we don't trust Jesus to forgive and heal us, we will never have the courage to rise up and take the next step. This may mean forgiving someone else, opening up to love again, pursuing a passion, taking steps in the direction of our dreams. We can think big. We can be free. We can pick up the stretchers of our brokenness and walk on.

Lord Jesus, help me rise up to follow you.

Kristin Armstrong

Be a Generous Giver

Whoever sows sparingly will also reap sparingly, and whoever sows bountifully will also reap bountifully. 2 Corinthians 9:6

Many people have helped me through difficult times in my life, either financially or by sowing the seeds of positive affirmation in my heart and soul. In whatever way they shared their bounty with me, the fruits of their generosity are visible in whom I have become, and whom I am still becoming, as I live in that love. When generosity is done out of love and without reservation or recompense, the fruits of that generosity replicate for the greater glory of God.

Generosity and graciousness that stem from the deepest part of one's heart is worth reflecting on: When have we reluctantly shared what we had but expected much more in return? When have we given to others for no other reason than to receive something in return—credit, recognition or praises? When have we given and expected nothing in return but received so much more? What has been your experience of giving, serving and emptying out without reservation?

Vivian Amu

'Work,' 'Labor,' 'Endurance'

We give thanks to God always…calling to mind your work of faith and labor of love and endurance in hope…

1 Thessalonians 1:2-3

I love the actions that are coupled here with the virtues of faith, hope and love. Paul calls faith "work." He refers to love as "labor." He says hope is an act of "endurance." These words suggest the gritty, roll-up-your-sleeves quality of discipleship emphasizing that it is an effort to believe. We believe consciously, repeatedly and with all of our might. Faith, hope and love are not fluffy, free-spirited qualities. They are arduous. Even hope is not just a breezy wishing for the best; it is an act of will—a decision to look for the movement of the Spirit, no matter how dark things seem. Sometimes it seems we can't do enough for our troubled world. After a lifetime of effort, things might even seem worse than when we started. It is an act of will to not become jaded, to not give up. Rather, we put our shoulder to the plow and continue marching toward God, the horizon that is always before us.

Lord, be with me in the work of discipleship.

Karla Manternach

An Age-old Love

With age-old love I have loved you; so I have kept my mercy toward you. Jeremiah 31:3

When the city of Jerusalem was invaded by the Assyrians in 587 B.C., great numbers of the citizens were forced to be exiled in Babylon. They hoped to be released and return home, but they were prisoners for many years. When freedom continued to be denied, the exiles began to question their faith, thinking that God did not love them, that he ignored their cries for help. It was then that Jeremiah was inspired to give courage and hope to his fellow exiled citizens. Eventually they were able to return home.

Thankfully, we are not prisoners in a foreign country. But we have our litanies of personal trials and many tragic happenings in the world. A common complaint can be heard questioning why God does not intervene on our behalf and protect us. The prophet's words can still resound through the ages to give us hope and courage, for we believe that God has promised to be merciful; we are loved with an "age-old love."

Fr. James McKarns

Always in the Boat

Jesus was in the stern, asleep on a cushion. They woke him and said to him, "Teacher, do you not care that we are perishing?" Mark 4:38

We might easily get annoyed when someone doesn't take a situation as seriously as we do. If we're worried, we want others to be worried right along with us. But when the apostles were panicking, fearing for their lives, Jesus was sound asleep! How could he be so calm about the situation? The apostles were experienced fishermen. No doubt they had passed through their share of storms, so they knew that this was a severe one. They knew that they couldn't handle the situation on their own. And so, they called on Jesus. The times that we most worry, when we panic and are most afraid, are usually the times when we have failed to put our faith in God. Jesus awoke and rescued the apostles.

No matter where we go, no matter what we're facing, let's not panic. Let's recall our faith and remember that Jesus is always in the boat with us.

Terence Hegarty

Healing the Wounds

**He heals the brokenhearted
and binds up their wounds.** Psalm 147:3

The wounds of divorce run deep. You wouldn't know it by the legal document issued as proof a civil marriage has ended. What's left are scraps of the past. For divorced Catholics, the prospect of then petitioning the Church for a declaration of nullity can be too much to bear. Who wants to revisit such pain? Why open old wounds? Because fragments of a failed marriage have a way of piercing the present and unnamed future. The Church, in its wisdom, understands that. I witness this as a field delegate for our local Tribunal. It takes nothing short of courage to seek a declaration of nullity. But this canonical process, as burdensome as it may seem, can be an instrument of peace and hope. To learn from the past and go forward with God's grace is a healing balm. The wounds of divorce need not fester in hearts yearning to be made whole.

Gail Goleas

243 Hopeful Devotions *for* Catholics

MARY, MOTHER OF HOPE

She gave birth to a son, a male child, destined to rule all the nations with an iron rod. Revelation 12:5

The Queenship of Mary—Pope Benedict XVI called it "a title of trust, of joy, and of love." Isn't that beautiful? Of course, the woman who bore, nursed and loved Jesus is worthy of such an august name.

As for ourselves, on most days we may not feel much like queens- or kings-in-the-making. But Mary is always there in our corner, lifting us up in the situations where we're tempted to lose hope, or in the sorrows that seem so unfair and insurmountable. It was faith that helped Mary persevere through Simeon's prophecy, through the three days the child Jesus was missing, through his crucifixion—and to the resurrection. She longs to intercede for us to embrace that same faith and trust, never more than during the times we feel devoid of hope. She longs to advocate for us for our place in heaven.

Hail, Holy Queen! Help me to live today in a way pleasing to you and your Son, the King.

Melanie Rigney

Courage, Hope, Faith

It is my choice to die at the hands of men with the hope God gives of being raised up by him. 2 Maccabees 7:14

This story from Maccabees has long held me in awe. It brings to mind words of Winston Churchill: "Fear is a reaction, courage is a decision." Quite clearly, these brothers had courage…along with hope and deep faith in God. Now that's a formidable combination! Reflecting on these traits, I ask myself, "Am I so committed to God as to die 'at the hands of men'?" In truth, I don't know that I'm made of the stuff of martyrs. What gives me hope are Paul's words to the Corinthians about the body being made of many parts, each vital to the whole. He then writes of how God has bestowed on us different gifts, but the same spirit, and each is vital to the Church. This leads me to conclude that regardless of our particular God-given gift, it is ours to use to bring about his Kingdom on earth. No comparisons needed, no guilt necessary.

Judy Schueneman

Eyes Wide Open

I believe that I shall see the bounty of the Lord in the land of the living. Psalm 27:13

"Seeing is believing," some insist. For people of faith like us, however, what we see confirms our faith. We pray to have eyes and hearts open to the ordinary miracles that make up our daily lives. Then we're able to see how God is actively bringing about resurrections in ordinary wonders, from seeds bursting forward new life to healing miracles. Since we see the world through the lens of faith, our faith also influences how we act. We respond to the suffering and injustices we see, trying to share hope with those in darkness and despair. We are compelled to generously give of ourselves and come to know Christ present among the poor in our midst. With eyes wide open to God's goodness, we can continue rejoicing in the wonders of our redemption, the wonder that proves that God's might is bigger than our fears and limitations.

God, help me to see the truth of who you are and act with great love.

Sr. Julia Walsh, F.S.P.A.

God Still Reigns

Abraham prostrated himself and laughed as he said to himself, "Can a child be born to a man who is a hundred years old? Can Sarah give birth at ninety?" Genesis 17:17

Have you experienced a moment like this with God? When something lines up or shows up for you that is so impossibly good that your response is *laughter*? Unmitigated delight, gratitude, wonder?

In these moments, we know that we know. There is no way we could have orchestrated or optimized anything this good. It's beyond comprehension, beyond our capacity to envision or construct. It's boundless in potential, reach, realm. It destroys all construct of fear or limitation. It feels like awe. Like love. Like power.

When humans don't know how to respond, we typically laugh or cry—and in the highest of moments, we usually do both at the same time.

Miracles are still in effect, still happening, still offered to us.

It's time to be open to the potential. Prepare to be overjoyed.

Kristin Armstrong

MATURING IN FAITH

Then the boy's father cried out, "I do believe, help my unbelief!" Mark 9:24

I used to think this was the prayer of someone young and immature in the ways of spiritual life, but I have come to understand why the prayer is uttered by the parent in the story. It takes some living, some failing and some hard-won humility to get to such an honest place. Faith is not certainty, and we will all face challenging unknowns in our life. It often takes years or even decades to see the good that came out of a difficult or painful experience. Until that time comes, it is really helpful to have people in our lives who allow us to express both our hope and our doubt. So often we rush to make ourselves feel better when someone faces suffering, so we fill the room with words when our silent prayerful presence is what is needed.

Terri Mifek

Breathing a Blessing

By the word of the LORD the heavens were made;
   by the breath of his mouth all their host. Psalm 33:6

Often our manner of breathing reveals something about our emotional state. When we're anxious or terrified, we may feel as if we're holding our breath or that our breathing is shallow and rapid. When we're feeling heavily burdened, our breath may be let out in one long, continuous sigh. When we're in a state of contentment, our breath may be described as even and peaceful.

The psalmist reveals what happens when God "breathes," a breath so centered, vibrant and generative that it creates new life and new possibility everywhere. It's an invitation for each of us to reflect on the blessings that should follow in the wake of every breath we take.

Loving God, may my breathing in and breathing out create a mindfulness of your presence in my life and in the lives of all I meet today.

Sr. Chris Koellhoffer, I.H.M.

Suffering, Yet Strong

From now on, let no one make troubles for me; for I bear the marks of Jesus on my body. Galatians 6:17

What makes us strong? Natural aspects of personality, undoubtedly, but circumstances do have something to do with it as well. After my husband died suddenly at the age of 50, over ten years ago, I found myself looking at life differently in many ways. Over time, one of those ways, it was clear, was a position of greater strength. After all I'd been through, what else could hurt me?

Paul is speaking of something different here, but perhaps we can still see a connection. In communion with Jesus, we are in communion with his wounds and suffering. But it doesn't end there, does it? For his wounds are rooted in love and point to eternal life. By holding on to him and accepting that suffering, love and hope in a healthy way, I'm changed. I'm strong.

Jesus, I look to you for strength in the face of today's challenges.

Amy Welborn

The Courage to Risk

Why is my pain continuous,
my wound incurable, refusing to be healed?

Jeremiah 15:18

Many of us have wondered the same thing as Jeremiah over the past couple of years. With greater uncertainty in our lives, possible threats to our futures, jobs lost, health diminished, all of a sudden, faith takes on a different face. It is easy to practice faith when everything is going well. It is harder to do so when everything is going wrong.

Jeremiah had the honesty to complain to God. God's promises didn't seem to materialize. They were rather like a cruel joke: "To me you are like a deceptive brook" (verse 18). God doesn't appear to be too concerned about what Jeremiah thinks of him. Instead, the Lord seeks to support Jeremiah in moving beyond the depression he is in. God offers the dispirited prophet not a miracle, but a covenant. In this situation, faith requires the courage to risk entering into partnership with God without seeing proofs of a future we prefer, trusting that he will indeed be with us.

Sr. Kathryn James Hermes, F.S.P.

'SEIZE THE HOPE SET BEFORE US'

We earnestly desire each of you to demonstrate the same eagerness for the fulfillment of hope… Hebrews 6:11

Two decades ago, when the disease of alcoholism had me by the throat, I felt both helpless and hopeless. I was hopeless because I thought I could stop drinking on my own, but I failed again and again. The first gift that Alcoholics Anonymous gave me as I heard people tell their stories at meetings was hope. If they could get sober, so could I. Moreover, they taught me to place my hope not in myself, but in "a Power greater than ourselves," who, if sought, could and would help us.

We often mistakenly assume we need to muster up enough virtue, enough hope—or faith or love—to deserve God's help. But we don't. Instead, we need to ask God's help in everything, including that our hope may be strengthened—our hope for ourselves, for others, for this desperate world of ours. And we need to encourage one another to, in the words of AA, "seize the hope set before us" in the steadfast promises of God.

Anonymous

AUGUST 30

A RESURGENCE OF LIFE

He stepped forward and touched the coffin; at this the bearers halted, and he said, "Young man, I tell you, arise!"

Luke 7:14

This call to life wasn't meant just for the young man in the coffin. The call is meant for us too. In our lives, God is constantly bringing newness of life from what is passing away. We die to our fears so that trust in God can be born. We die to selfishness so that love can be born. And finally, we die to life in this world so that we can be born into resurrected life. You can see the pattern here. God is always at work, bringing a resurgence of life for us from what has gone before. It brings us joy when we reflect on how God has done this for us all through our lives.

Lord, may I not be afraid to let go of what must pass away. Fill me with the faith and trust that can come only from you.

Fr. Kenneth E. Grabner, C.S.C.

House Call

> Consider it all joy, my brothers, when you encounter various trials, for you know that the testing of your faith produces perseverance. James 1:2-3

I dropped my head into my hands praying, "Lord, you've got to send me someone; you know I'm struggling." A week later, a repairman knelt fixing my washer. "I know one thing," he said. "You have a real love for Jesus in your heart."

I stammered. Yes, I loved Jesus. But a hard move, replete with trial and transition, left me despairing. I needed hope.

Seeing my conflicted face, the repairman asked me to open my Bible to the verses above. He encouraged me to persevere. This man had once nearly died. He promised that if he ever left the hospital, he'd read the Bible daily. His sharing of his faith awakened my hope. Having restored my washing machine and my hope, the man said goodbye.

I closed the door, laughing aloud and praising God for the unexpected house call. He'd sent a "repaired-man" to repair what was most needed within me.

Thank you, Lord, for encouraging us persevere while sending hope in unexpected ways.

Kathleen Swartz McQuaig

WORDS FOR TROUBLED HEARTS

Do not let your hearts be troubled… In my Father's house there are many dwelling places. John 14:1-2

This Gospel message is very special to me: it was the Gospel my family chose for my father's funeral. We chose this Gospel because we found it immensely consoling—especially those first words: "Do not let your hearts be troubled." When Dad died, our hearts were troubled—deeply troubled. We were troubled by the months of pain and uncertainty that had preceded his death. We were troubled by the loss of such a good man, such a significant person in all of our lives. We were troubled by our concern for our mother who had been married to Dad for almost 66 years. What would happen to her now? How would she survive without him?

Sometimes our expressions of faith coincide perfectly with what we are experiencing. Other times, our words at are odds with what we are thinking and how we are feeling. At such times, we must keep praying our words of faith, trusting that our experience, in due time, will catch up to our words.

Loving God, help me to keep praying words of faith even when my thoughts and feelings fall short of my words.

Sr. Melannie Svoboda, S.N.D.

SEEK HIM

The LORD's are the earth and its fullness…
Who can ascend the mountain of the LORD? Psalm 24:1, 3

We know that the expanding edge of the universe is many billions of lightyears distant—and that tiny earth is nowhere near the center of it all. Our knowledge does not make the psalmist's words any less true, just more amazing. Not only is the earth the Lord's, so is the vast universe to its farthest limits. As our picture of the universe has become enlarged, so has our sense of the God who created and sustains it. The greater God becomes, the deeper the mystery of his invitation to us to enter his presence.

Seek God, receive his blessings, the psalmist later urges his listeners in verses 5 and 6. His words continue to urge us today. No matter how powerful, how incomprehensible, how wise God is, seek him, come before him, receive the life he wishes to give. Let the vastness of his creation inspire not hesitation but awe.

Kevin Perrotta

The Answer Is Christ

Always be ready to give an explanation to anyone who asks you for a reason for your hope... 1 Peter 3:15

"Why are you so happy?" I hear people ask this when they don't know what to make of my joy and optimism. "Why are you so different?" What are my reasons for behaving as I do? What is the source of my hope and joy?

The answer is Christ. I love God. God loves me. I feel this and know it deeply, and it frames my identity and the way I take in life. This doesn't mean that I haven't dealt with intense hardships and suffering. Yet, even when life is heavy and full of struggle, my main habit is to hope and notice beauty. When it comes to God's goodness, I will not tire in my sense of wonder, and I know this provides my inspiration and motivation. God's love gives me direction.

Because you love God, do people notice that you're different? What is your inspiration and motivation for having hope?

Sr. Julia Walsh, F.S.P.A.

Nowhere Better to Turn

Simon Peter answered him, "Master, to whom shall we go? You have the words of eternal life." John 6:68

To live long, rich and fulfilling lives, we turn to many different kinds of people. We turn to our parents and teachers to instruct us in what we need to succeed and prosper. We turn to doctors and other scientists to guide us toward healthy lives. Perhaps we look to inspirational writers and speakers to point us toward more interesting, successful and ethical lives. These people can be a blessing.

But none of them—however beneficial—can offer what only God can give through a life in Christ. It's good to reach our fullest potential, but only God can give us life beyond this all-too-fleeting moment in time, however fulfilling it has been.

To whom else can we turn? Only to you, Jesus.

Steve Givens

To Know Him

> [Martha] came to him and said, "Lord, do you not care that my sister has left me by myself to do the serving? Tell her to help me." Luke 10:40

As a young adult, I spent a year as a full-time volunteer at an emergency outreach center. I worked hard there—and felt rather pious and important because of it. One busy day as I flew about helping people, a homeless man started following me around to talk about God. "Why did God make you?" he asked me. I flipped through the partial catechism in my brain and came up with, "To love and serve him." "No," the man admonished gently. "To know him, love him and serve him. You have to know him first."

And there it was: I was Martha, with full-blown do-stuff-for-Jesus syndrome. Certainly, we are called to serve the Lord by loving and serving one another. But it's possible to get so caught up in being worker bees for Jesus that we neglect other aspects of our faith life, like prayer and exploring God's Word.

Lord, I want to get to work. Help me remember to sit at your feet as well.

Karla Manternach

Dialogue With the Spirit

He does not ration his gift of the Spirit. John 3:34

I've often thought that the greatest blasphemy against the Holy Spirit is to deny Its power. Every now and then, I experience what I like to define as a "God event"—a profound revelation from Scripture, a way of seeing my circumstances in a new light that allows me to carry on with renewed hope. Sometimes a friend will repeat something I told them in a past moment of spiritual enlightenment, and it's as though I'm hearing it for the first time, like God saved the light to be returned to me when I really needed it.

Each event is a little thing that could be explained as a coincidence, but why not give our hearts permission to Glory in the mystery of God? Why not suspend doubt and allow that all things are working for God's purpose? Every conversation, interaction and encounter with the Word can be a colloquy with the Spirit of God.

Elizabeth Duffy

Mary, Our Hope

Can a mother forget her infant…
I will never forget you. Isaiah 49:15

A universal image of unconditional love is that of a mother. She looks at her children with an affection that is unique and unconditional, no matter how they have sinned.

Mary reminds us of this "maternal" love of God. While we rightly address God as Father, we are reminded of God's unconditional love as we gaze on the face of our heavenly Mother.

Thus do we look to Mary our Mother and address her as "our life, our sweetness and our hope." No matter how far we have fallen, in this heavenly Mother, we have a sure hope.

Mary, Mother of God and my Mother, I know you will never forget me. Reach down to your child and raise me up, so that I might live forever in the radiant presence of God.

Msgr. Stephen J. Rossetti

From the Heart

I will place my law within them, and write it upon their hearts.
Jeremiah 31:33

Jeremiah knows the intimacy God desires to have with us. God's law, written upon every heart, endures all things, has no barriers and knows no limits. It reaches beyond the legalities of right and wrong. God speaks to Jeremiah of a new covenant, a relationship based on unconditional love, given to the people of God despite their failings. This intimate relationship dwells within each of us. God has placed within us the desire to love even when loving hurts. The Gospels reveal exactly what God has written on our hearts. To act according to God's law is to love unconditionally. God's law means to forgive always, to give compassion when we've been offended and to restore unity wherever we find separation. And despite human failures to love, we have hope in God's enduring law. Our intimacy with God means trusting in God's forgiveness.

Deborah A. Meister

Don't Carry It Alone

I cannot carry all this people by myself, for they are too heavy for me. Numbers 11:14

Dissatisfied, whining people complaining about the manna, wanting meat instead! Poor Moses! It reminds me of my grandson: "But Grandma, I don't like orange cheese, only white!" Moses is at the end of his rope and ready to give up. Do you ever feel this way about the people God has given you to love? Why are they always inventing drama? Can't they just keep things simple and be satisfied?

For me the key message in this verse lies in the phrase "by myself." We too often try to solve people's problems, thinking we must order their lives and keep them happy. We try to manage everything ourselves. Read on. God gives Moses the solution: Assemble the seventy elders. You don't have to do this alone.

Today, take all the muttering people and their thorny problems to the Lord. He will guide you. It will work out.

Lord, help me to remember to go to you first with all the struggles of this life.

Jennifer Christ

'Hope for Glory'

It is Christ in you, the hope for glory. Colossians 1:27

On this day, we hold in ourselves the memory and present reality of suffering. On every day of the year, somebody carries a suffering: an anniversary of death, maybe the loss of innocence or health, of a love or of a job. These sufferings are real, and we can't just delete them, though we may find ourselves burying or escaping them for a while. What, then, can we do? Give up? Inflict pain on someone else, or more pain on ourselves? Run forever? Christ carves out another way—Paul points out—not a way out of suffering, but a way in suffering. Within us is hope. Hope, as Pope Francis has pointed out, is worked out with our hands, in the flesh. It is not mere optimism or positive thinking, but "hope for glory," the radiance and life of God-with-us. We can give God flesh in everything we do. Isn't that glorious?

Mary Marrocco

Glorious Grace

Therefore, we are not discouraged; rather, although our outer self is wasting away, our inner self is being renewed day by day. 2 Corinthians 4:16

In our day-to-day living, it's fairly easy to notice the "outer self... wasting away" in the gradual diminishment of aging, in the letting go of the way we looked in our youth, in the things we once could do with minimal effort. This realization may also appear if we struggle with lifelong illness, with the ravages of chronic pain or in noticing subtle changes in our body or energy.

But these signs of the inroads of time ought not discourage us, writes St. Paul, for no matter what the external appearances may be, there's a whole lot of glorious grace at work renewing and restoring our world from within. Every day, even when and perhaps especially when we feel the absence of what we once were or what we once could do, our spirit, blessed by God's grace and our own deep, inner soul work, is being transformed.

Holy One, help me to see, beyond appearances, your healing presence in my life.

Sr. Chris Koellhoffer, I.H.M.

Journeying on the Path

You will show me the path to life... Psalm 16:11

At a very early age, my mother taught me to ask God for guidance and direction at the beginning of each day. Together, we would pray the Morning Offering and dedicate to God all our prayers, works, joys and sufferings of that day. In that prayer, I was asking God, like the psalmist of old, to show me the path of life. Now that I have acquired the title of octogenarian, I look back on how I have traveled those many years with my morning offering sentiments. I've traveled highways and low ways, fast ways and slow ways, but always with Jesus on my mind. Now I think more about the path than the road. Today, I choose a slower pace, a pace at which I can walk and pause to enjoy the creative beauty of nature around me. On roads, we often hurry from place to place. But on the path, we can just enjoy the journey. I hope and trust that we all can walk with grace and dignity on our paths to the eternal Kingdom.

Fr. James McKarns

All Jesus

For I resolved to know nothing while I was with you except Jesus Christ, and him crucified. 1 Corinthians 2:2

Let me tell you about all the crosses in my house. In the living room, there's the simple, yet vivid crucifix from Mexico. In the next room hangs a brightly painted ceramic cross, swirling with primary colors, from Sicily. Look on the shelf, and we're back in Mexico—a small crucifix completely woven from palm branches—a Palm Sunday tradition there. In my room, I look near my desk and I see the plain wooden cross, part of the monk-made casket in which my husband was buried. The cross was on the lid and fashioned to be removed and kept above ground by those still here. And over there by the door is the Risen Christ—odd considering how traditional my mother was—that was my First Communion gift decades ago. All different, all the same. All Jesus, in suffering and love, with me on this journey always.

Amy Welborn

Mary, Faithful Mother at Calvary

Behold, your mother. John 19:27

No healthy person likes to suffer. Perhaps just as bad as physical suffering is the thought of suffering alone. Perhaps that explains the growth of support groups for people who are undergoing difficulties. These groups, by enlisting the presence and support of others, can be positive ways of enduring hard times.

The image of Jesus on the Cross is meant to tell us that God, too, understands our suffering. Like Jesus, we may feel abandoned by God during our darkest hour, but we are never really abandoned. God supports us and endures the crosses of our lives with us.

But the Christian life offers us yet another consolation in our suffering. In this Gospel, we hear Jesus giving us, in the person of John, Mary to be our mother: "Behold, your mother." In that act, Mary became the mother of all.

Just as Jesus was not abandoned on the Cross by his mother, so neither are we abandoned by her. As Mary faithfully kneels at the foot of Jesus' Cross, so does she stay close to us in our need. "Our Lady of Sorrows" is a sure support during the Calvary of our lives.

Msgr. Stephen J. Rossetti

September 15

A Childlike Faith

Let the children come to me. Mark 10:14

It has to be one of my fondest childhood images of Jesus. Seated among a group of children, a smiling Jesus beckons the children to his side. I believed then what my parents told me, what Sister taught us and what Father said from the pulpit. This young man in the flowing robes with the kind face loved us and wanted us to be good, to help others, to pray and to love God. It seemed so simple then.

And yet in this same Gospel, Jesus cautions us to retain a child-like faith if we are to enter heaven. There is nothing wrong in our search for rational explanations. God gave us that ability. But faith—the faith of a child—is based on love and trust and hope. It is that kind of faith that Jesus is asking us as grown-ups to retain from our youth. It's still a simple message of love of God and love of our neighbor. There is no need to complicate it, no pretense, no complex rationalizations. Jesus beckons the adults too.

Paul Pennick

A Prosperity
of the Soul

**The father of orphans and the defender of widows
is God in his holy dwelling.** Psalm 68:6

There are late-night televangelists who preach a "gospel of prosperity." They promise (especially if you send a donation) that if your faith in God is strong enough, you will be blessed in ways that will make you successful and powerful. While I have no doubt that God can work through us in any way he chooses, I don't believe that the "power of my faith" affects my wealth and social standing.

What God can and does give us is an inner peace based on what we really need. Our strength in life comes not from telling God to give us what we think we need, but rather from depending on God to give us our daily bread. My life is good. I think I have all that I need and then some. But I glory in the fact that my God is also the God of orphans, widows and the poor—those who might have less but who receive the same measure of inner peace and strength that only God can deliver.

God, be the provider of prosperity for my soul.

Steve Givens

September 17

Second Chances

Sir, leave it for this year also, and I shall cultivate the ground around it and fertilize it; it may bear fruit in the future. If not you can cut it down. Luke 13:8-9

The landowner comes out to his fig tree in hopes of gathering fruit. And, finding none, he instructs the gardener to cut the tree down. It is, after all, exhausting the soil and offering nothing in return. The gardener asks him to have a bit more patience. He offers to help cultivate and fertilize the tree and see what happens. If it is still barren after that, then okay, we'll go ahead and chop it down, the gardener says. This is exactly the offering made to God by Jesus on behalf of our sinful nature and our selfish, barren seasons. Jesus asks God to be patient and merciful while he works on us and with us. Tenderly, he helps us cultivate our lives so that we can truly become productive and abundant. We are all part of the planting, the fertilizing and the harvest. Let's cooperate with the Gardener.

Kristin Armstrong

SOARING LIKE AN EAGLE

They that hope in the LORD will renew their strength, they will soar on eagles' wings. Isaiah 40:31

Two things impressed me about this verse from Isaiah. First, the word "hope." Hope is the virtue that carries our faith and love into the future. The future, however, is the great unknown. As such, it can be scary (that's why we buy insurance!). But this verse tells us in whom we place our hope for the future—not in ourselves, not in some guru, not in a particular program or prayer, not even in a certain church leader. No, we place our hope in the Lord, in God. The second thing that impresses me in this verse is the image of the eagle. For a moment, picture in your mind an eagle soaring in the air high above the earth. How does an eagle soar? Seemingly effortlessly, and with strength, perseverance and grace. Those are the qualities that we, too, will have if we, indeed, place our hope in God.

Creating God, help me to place my hope in you. Then give me the strength, perseverance and grace to help bring about the better future for which I hope.

Sr. Melannie Svoboda, S.N.D.

HOPEFUL PRAYER

Ask and it will be given to you. Matthew 7:7

Of all the words in the Gospel that make me say, "O Lord, I want to believe!" these are foremost. Jesus is telling his disciples not to lose hope as they pray. I firmly believe in the necessity of prayer; it is as essential as breathing. I believe in its power; I've personally witnessed God's astonishing response to prayer.

And still I lose hope. Still I come back to God with the same prayer I've been praying for fifteen years, wondering who's more tired of this petition, God or me. Is it time to give up? Have I been praying for the wrong thing? Has God been saying, "No," and it just hasn't gotten through to me? It's not supposed to be about whether I deserve it, so my sins and failings can't be the problem—can they?

Into this desert of doubt comes the soft rain of Jesus' love. Ask. Search. Knock. No "best before date" is given, no stipulation made as to the type of petition or quality of prayer. Simply God's word. Since Christ himself is God's Word, it cannot fail. The Word is made flesh. This is as true for you and me as it was for the first disciples.

Lord, I dare to ask, for you have promised.

Mary Marrocco

Freely Given Gift

Why does he eat with tax collectors and sinners? Mark 2:16

Yes, Jesus shared his precious time with tax collectors and sinners—and this is the best news we could ever hope to get! Think about it. If Jesus could love them, then surely he can love us. No matter what mistakes we make, Jesus' love for us never changes. That might be hard to understand. Many people think of love as something we have to earn, but we can never earn God's love. God's love is a divine energy constantly being poured into us as a freely given gift. We can't change that no matter what we do because we can never change God. Rather, it is God's love that changes us. God's love has the power to transform our life. It helps us to seek reconciliation and vow to sin no more. It helps us to love and forgive ourselves and others as well. Can you imagine the kind of world we would have if more people decided to do that?

Fr. Kenneth E. Grabner, C.S.C.

ROOTED IN HOPE

Rejoice in hope, endure in affliction, and persevere in prayer.
Romans 12:12

I love watching trees through the seasons. To me, trees represent endurance, perseverance, trust and hope. Even when they are riddled with disease, bent over by strong winds or burned by fire, they often remain rooted to the ground. It takes a lot to topple one. Now, isn't that endurance?

Even when no one pays any attention to them or stops to water their roots or prune their dead branches, they still stand tall, as if they know God wouldn't let them down. They don't fall if there is no rain for one day to water their roots. Now, isn't that perseverance?

In autumn and into winter, everything seems taken from the trees during the colder months—they are stripped of their leaves, flowers, colors. Still, it won't be long before they rise again, rejoicing with new leaves, flowers, branches and the blessings of spring. Now, that's what I call a lesson in hope.

Loving God, may your gift of trees be an example for us to continuously place our trust in you.

Vivian Amu

Never Alone

But I am not alone, because the Father is with me. I have told you this so that you might have peace in me. John 16:32-33

Jesus knew most of his followers would scatter when it mattered most, afraid to be seen with him because their own lives could be at risk. He knew he would be isolated. And that is a feeling with which we as humans are all too familiar. Perhaps the person we loved most in the world has died, or a trusted friend has betrayed us, or we feel misled by someone who provided what we thought was good advice. We guard our hearts rather than trusting again, and we feel so alone.

That feeling is understandable. Other humans always will let us down, often unintentionally. But their failings and our own need not rob us of the peace that surpasses all understanding. Jesus held on to that peace, offering prayers to God even as he breathed his last. He showed us we are never truly alone, and no one can snatch peace from us.

How can you find peace today in a situation that threatens to isolate you?

Melanie Rigney

God's Goodness to Us

Give thanks to the Lord, for he is good,
  for his mercy endures forever;
Give thanks to the God of gods,
  for his mercy endures forever;
Give thanks to the Lord of lords,
  for his mercy endures forever. Psalm 136:1-3

If you open your Bible to Psalm 136, you'll read that refrain—"his mercy endures forever"—twenty-six times! This psalm of thanksgiving extols God's majestic work in Creation and his faithful love throughout Israel's history. It keeps alive the memory of the goodness of God. How important this is for us too.

I wonder what we might learn if we took the psalmist's approach—and wrote a brief twenty-six-line history of our lives punctuated by the constant refrain of God's forever mercy? It might become our own prayer inviting God's mercy to speak his goodness and steadfast love over all of it, over our memories of good or ill.

Lord, help me to better trust you in all the circumstances of my life.

Pat Gohn

Rethinking My To-Do List

> **For I know well the plans I have in mind for you…plans for your welfare and not for woe, so as to give you a future of hope.** Jeremiah 29:11

My morning prayer is often cluttered with my concerns about tasks. Then at night I see that I only achieved a fraction of what I hoped. The pattern is practically hilarious because each day I am reminded that I am not in charge. Rather, I am God's instrument—and God's plans matter most.

I am slowly learning that God's plans are for communal welfare, not individual prosperity. The plans God has for my days—and life—are not about *my* success, but about the flourishing of the common good of my neighbors.

St. Augustine wrote, "Hope has two beautiful daughters; their names are Anger and Courage. Anger at the way things are, and Courage to see that they do not remain as they are."

How different could my to-do list be if I planned with that type of hope?

Sr. Julia Walsh, F.S.P.A.

September 25

Looking for the Blessing

Trust in the Lord and do good... Psalm 37:3

It was our 50th wedding anniversary, and we were under a stay-at-home order due to the COVID-19 pandemic. I felt a wave of disappointment as I gazed at the tickets to the dinner theatre we had purchased months ago. Before the day had ended, however, we had been showered with our favorite wine, received well wishes in chalk on our driveway from our grandchildren and miraculously received the missing ingredient I needed to make a special dinner. It was not the day we envisioned, but it was still a day filled with gifts.

Like so many, I experienced losses and disappointments during the pandemic—minor compared to some but difficult nonetheless. I was reminded again that in times of seeming abandonment, the ability to see God working through others makes the difference between feeling despair or hope.

How has God been present to you in times of suffering? How have you been the presence of Christ to others?

Terri Mifek

THE UNEARNED WAGE

...These last ones worked only one hour, and you have made them equal to us, who bore the day's burden and the heat.

Matthew 20:12

My teen and I came across this passage during a recent Bible study. Her reaction was visceral. I could actually see the indignation in her posture. I get it. She wants the world to be fair. She wants everyone to do their part and get their just reward. I want that too. Yet this passage, more than any other in Scripture, fills me with hope in the Lord's promise of eternal life. I know that I am sinful and unable to make myself worthy of heaven. I keep trying, of course. We all should, but this parable suggests that God's mercy and generosity exceed our poor power to improve ourselves. In the end, heaven is a gift, freely given to us by a loving God. It is the full day's wage we need but cannot earn.

Have mercy on me, Lord, and grant me eternal life!

Karla Manternach

Hiding in Plain Sight

Have you seen him whom my heart loves?

Song of Songs 3:3

"Where's my cell phone?" It's a question I ask too often. Did it slip out of my pocket? Chances are it's probably right where I left it. Wherever that is. I panic. Was it stolen? Will I find it? I retrace my steps, reminding myself a phone cannot walk away. We convince ourselves we'd be lost without those cell phones because we rely on them so much.

In those moments when I feel abandoned and ask myself where God is, the answer lies within my own heart. No one can steal God away from me...or you. If his presence is lacking in our lives, it's because we get lost in our own distractions—cell phones included.

God never leaves us. Ever. God is always ready to be found. No internet connection needed. No password required.

Let us seek the Lord, for he will be found!

Gail Goleas

MY 'ANGEL OF PRAYER'

Is anyone among you suffering? He should pray. Is anyone in good spirits? He should sing praise. James 5:13

We are asked to pray when we are suffering, to sing when we are in good spirits. If our loved ones are sick, we are to call in faith-filled people. Our joy and sorrow, our sickness and health, can be living prayers if we allow ourselves to taste our experiences.

Whether suffering or in good spirits, let us turn to the One who companions both our broken and joyful hearts. We ought never underestimate the power of prayer, even when it appears that nothing is happening, that God has gone to the Bahamas for all we know. Then it's time to believe that every prayer has its own guardian angel. Sometimes the angel of prayer cradles us with tenderness and anoints us with the oil of patience and hope. At other times, the angel of prayer skips along beside us, lifting our spirits higher, that we may discover an even deeper joy.

O Angel of Prayer, inspire me to pray always. Guide me through all of life that I may experience God's presence in sickness and in health, in times of suffering, in times of happiness. Teach me that there is no such thing as a lost prayer.

Sr. Macrina Wiederkehr, O.S.B.

SEPTEMBER 29

Tried and True

No one has ever seen God. Yet, if we love one another, God remains in us, and his love is brought to perfection in us.

1 John 4:12

When John, the beloved apostle, was advanced in age, he preached a message consisting of only five words: "Little children, love one another." He had distilled the wisdom of his many years of Christian living into this brief message. Most likely John was simply restating the words of Jesus, who had told the crowds they needed to become like little children to enter the Kingdom of heaven. It is easy to see the divine love and beauty of God in the face, eyes and trusting ways of a little child.

To improve our love for one another and strengthen the presence of God within us, we don't need to find new and exotic religious practices. We need only to remember that innocent, trusting love we had as children and then replicate that in our adult lives.

Fr. James McKarns

'My Reward Is With the Lord'

Though I thought I had toiled in vain,
  for nothing and for naught spent my strength,
Yet my reward is with the Lord... Isaiah 49:4

As we celebrate the feast of St. Thérèse of Lisieux, we may be consoled in remembering that her life, like ours, was not without experiences of doubt and wondering if her life had had meaning. As a Carmelite, she was not confined by the boundaries of the cloister, but instead opened her heart to a worldview that prayed for people across the globe. Her spiritual practice was called the "Little Way," living with attentiveness to the presence of the Holy in the everyday.

Surely, we might think that, as she faced death at a tender age, she would have been consoled by her good works. Instead, she was wracked with terror and something close to despair by the overwhelming feeling that her life had been useless. In her hours of torment, she clung to the conviction that her recompense was with a loving, forgiving God.

Holy One, look at my life with the eyes of your compassionate love.

Sr. Chris Koellhoffer, I.H.M.

Surrounded by Saints and Angels

You are fellow citizens with the holy ones. Ephesians 2:19

When our earthly pursuits become separated from the reality of our eternal citizenship, we are soon in a crisis of hope. We fall for the illusion that we are alone, individuals struggling against a hostile environment. As I write this, one of my sisters is dying. This evening she is very near the end. She says she can see her guardian angel in the room.

We are never alone. We walk together through life with all the saints and angels surrounding us and cheering us on. Many saints have experienced the sufferings and joys that fill your particular life. Your guardian angel surrounds you with care and protection, guarding you safely to the moment when you will enter heaven to be drawn into the eternal love in the heart of God. We don't have to wait until the end of our life to know that we are surrounded by the holy ones with whom we are meant to share our life. That will be a graced moment when our faith will be rewarded with sight. So strengthen your faith today and keep walking toward eternity.

Sr. Kathryn James Hermes, F.S.P.

Dealing With the Curve

Behold, we are going up to Jerusalem, and the Son of Man will be handed over to the chief priests and the scribes, and they will condemn him to death... Matthew 20:18

Life has a way of throwing us curveballs. Just when everything is humming along, we lose a job, a friend dies suddenly or the institutions we trusted fail us. We may feel lost and angry. Encountering unexpected difficulties will test us, just as the first disciples were tested as they faced the death of their beloved friend and teacher. When things look hopeless, that is simply a challenge, one that, ideally, will prompt us to see the situation through the eyes of faith. We want our wishes to be fulfilled, but we live in a world that we often can't control. However, our faith calls us to trust that God is at work within and around us. As we struggle with our unbelief, it is comforting to know that even our doubts can be transformative if they make us more compassionate, humble and honest followers of Christ.

Terri Mifek

ST. FRANCIS OF ASSISI

**Help us, O God our savior,
  because of the glory of your name.** Psalm 79:9

Francis, go and rebuild my Church, which is falling into ruins! St. Francis heard these words as he prayed before the Crucifix in the church of San Damiano. He took the words literally and began repairing the church building with the help of his friends. Only later did he realize that Jesus was asking him to rebuild the *spiritual* life of the Church.

After the assassination of Robert Kennedy, the mayor of San Francisco asked people to voluntarily turn in their guns, which were then melted down to form the statue. Sculptor Beniamino "Benny" Bufano (1890-1970) created a nine-foot-tall metal statue of St. Francis, still standing near its city college, a lasting reminder of Francis' passion to make peace among all people through love and non-violence. Our challenge today is to do whatever we can to rebuild, renew and strengthen our Church so that it will be a sign of hope and an instrument of peace for all peoples and nations.

Lord, make me an instrument of your peace.

Fr. Martin Pable, O.F.M. Cap.

Trust in God's Fidelity

For I am convinced that neither death, nor life, nor angels, nor principalities, nor present things, nor future things, nor powers, nor height, nor depth, nor any other creature will be able to separate us from the love of God in Christ Jesus our Lord.

Romans 8:38-39

Do you find there are some Scripture passages you have reached for in hard times so often that one day you realize you know them by heart? These verses from Paul's letter to the Romans are ones for me. His wording is so powerful, his rhetoric building in intensity phrase by phrase, it has seemed to me he might have been hanging on to it himself—perhaps in beatings, shipwreck, prison or terrible regret for his persecution of Christians. I have said these words aloud to myself in many kinds of personal darkness, and sometimes just as strongly for someone else—a seriously troubled loved one or someone I hear about in danger on the news. The heart of all hope: *nothing* can separate us from God's love.

Patricia Livingston

No More Death

He will wipe every tear from their eyes, and there shall be no more death or mourning, wailing or pain, for the old order has passed away. Revelation 21:4

I think I was just eight or nine when a favorite uncle died and, in small steps of understanding, I began to see that there is an order to life. And somewhere in that order, I was promised something different and eternal.

Death stings, no matter our age. We miss those gone from us. We grieve lives taken too soon. Death is meant to hurt, for in anticipation of those losses, we find what is most precious to us. We figure out who and how to love. But a time will come, we are promised, when the tables will be turned. Death will no longer sting. The order we have come to know will pass away. And when that happens, we will meet the God who is love.

Hold me when I grieve and give me hope, Lord, until the time for grieving ends.

Steve Givens

Rock of Ages

Be my rock of refuge,
a stronghold to give me safety,
for you are my rock and my fortress. Psalm 71:3

The psalmist uses "rock" to evoke divine security, stability and permanence. And "rock" as a symbol for God or eternity has been used often through the ages.

There was a stark reminder recently that even this classic symbol can fail us. The famous granite cliff profile "Old Man of the Mountain" near Franconia, NH (which I saw some years back), eventually collapsed into a pile of rubble. It was a sad occasion in New England, even though the rock formation was so fragile that cables, cement and epoxy had been used for decades to try to anchor it.

I don't suppose we will ever get over the tendency to overinvest in what looks stable but isn't. Surely there's a lesson to learn when even our most trusted metaphors fail us. Yes, we want God to be our "rock," but we have to let our faith and hope define the kind of "rock" God must be for us. Our spiritual safety may not rest so much in clinging to what seems solid and immobile, but in going with the flow of grace that may seem a lot more like a runaway canoe going down the rapids than the granite cliffs piercing the sky above.

James E. Adams

October 7

Leading Us Toward God

Whenever unclean spirits saw him they would fall down before him and shout, "You are the Son of God." Mark 3:11

What is a conscience? As I reflected on this question, it occurred to me that a conscience is not supposed to just make us feel bad, but also should guide us toward the right path—the unclean spirits seemingly recognized this. What if we altered our perspective and thought of our conscience in this way—leading us to God and to moral truth as well as highlighting where we have made mistakes? Would this not make listening to our conscience more appealing and helpful? This perspective could help us see our conscience as a helpful voice rather than a harsh critic. Our faith invites us to open our conscience to the presence of Jesus for healing and transformation, and to recognize him as the loving Son of God. To do this, we might have to recalibrate our moral compass. Befriending our conscience could help us recognize the presence of the holy in our lives and encourage us to move toward God rather than cowering away in fear.

David Nantais

Turning to the Lord

I love you, O Lord, my strength,
    O Lord, my rock, my fortress, my deliverer.
My God, my rock of refuge,
    my shield, the horn of my salvation, my stronghold!

Psalm 18:2-3

These words were uttered during a mountaintop moment of faith. David just narrowly escaped the clutches of his enemies and was delivered by none other than the Almighty: "my cry to him reached his ears" (verse 7). In our moments of distress, where do we turn? To a friend? To the phone? To food? To a glass of wine? Inward? Off?

We must train ourselves in less significant, everyday moments to turn first to the Lord. By practicing this behavior in ordinary times, it becomes a reflex action when things take an extraordinary turn. This training could be what saves us, like David, in our moment of peril. We call on God first. We thank him immediately and openly.

"He set me free in the open, and he rescued me, because he loves me" (verse 20). He loves you too, and he will rescue you in your moment of need. Call on him.

Kristin Armstrong

CROSSES AND OPPORTUNITIES

We ourselves boast of you in the churches of God regarding your endurance and faith in all your persecutions and the afflictions you endure. 2 Thessalonians 1:4

One of the fundamental characteristics of authentic Christian faith is its tendency to see hard times, stressful situations and outright suffering of all kinds as both a cross and an opportunity. When we are afflicted, regardless of the cause, we pray for courage, patience and the grace to endure. But we also see such experiences as an opportunity to deepen our faith and trust in God, who invites us, nay insists, that we relate to him as our always-loving Father. No matter how dark our situation, no matter how afflicted we may be, no matter how hard the times we cannot avoid, our faith calls us to endure and to trust that our loving Father is involved here too, and hope is always appropriate.

Lord Jesus, help me to endure hard times and always be hopeful.

Mitch Finley

TRUE PRAYER

I will bless the LORD at all times;
  his praise shall be ever in my mouth. Psalm 34:2

It is important that our prayers be honest and truthful. It is so easy to praise God when things go our way, a family member is healed, or our new job peeks over the horizon. But what happens when God asks us to wait, or even says "No"? Do we place a no-care onus on the Divine?

Blessing means to accept the hopeful fact that God may have a surprise in store that is infinitely more than we dare expect, and to surrender to God's plan, believing without a doubt that God cares for us and loves us beyond all telling. With praise on our lips, can we leave the outcome of our fervent prayers in God's hands and Christ's heart?

Sr. Bridget Haase, O.S.U.

Add the Leaven

A little yeast leavens the whole batch of dough. Galatians 5:9

If you've ever baked bread from scratch, you know the yeast is the key ingredient in the whole enterprise. The ability to "raise up" the mixture is what makes flour and water into bread.

We all seem to be adept at dragging things down with our criticisms, judgments, negativity and even complaints about the weather. Yet it's more creative and challenging to be the leaven— to find the proverbial silver lining, the divine essence or the ray of hope that raises up a situation. It takes only a small amount of yeast to get good action going. It could merely be your smile, a friendly joke or a remark like, "Hey, you look great today!"

The whole lump of this life needs us to be working like yeast to build the Kingdom!

Lord, when it all looks so dull like just flour and water, help me to be the leaven that turns this day into a golden, fragrant loaf.

Jennifer Christ

Faithful—Moment to Moment

Take care, brothers, that none of you may have an evil and unfaithful heart, so as to forsake the living God. Encourage yourselves daily while it is still "today," so that none of you may grow hardened by the deceit of sin. Hebrews 3:12-13

This passage urges us to "live in the now"—a trendy idea, and also an ancient one. It calls us to open our hearts to God, be faithful to him and guard against evil. We are to choose God every day, watching out for the hardness that comes from thinking, *I can forgive later, when I'm good and ready. I can do the right thing later, when I have more time. I can help my neighbors later because they will still be there.*

Discipleship is a lifelong endeavor, but it is lived out one choice at a time. Our fidelity to God takes place moment to moment, day to day. It expresses itself in our decisions, large and small, and in doing the right thing now while we still have the chance.

Gracious God, help me be faithful while it is still today.

Karla Manternach

October 13

God's Faithfulness

The Lord is good:
his kindness endures forever,
and his faithfulness, to all generations. Psalm 100:5

These words ring true for me whenever I think of the major events that have made my life what it is, the schools to which I was sent, the development of my vocation, the people who influenced my life: All of these were God's gifts, signs of God's enduring love. And when I reflect on the mistakes I might have made were it not for God's guidance, I realize that God's faithfulness has upheld me throughout my entire life.

Perhaps many of us might have similar thoughts if we recalled the past events of our lives. The reminiscences would bring us joy as we reflected on how God's faithfulness has been with us throughout the various stages of our lives. And God's fidelity in the past is a promise of his fidelity in the future.

Lord, may I remember your faithfulness that has made me who I am. I thank you for your love that has touched all the parts of my life.

Fr. Kenneth E. Grabner, C.S.C.

COME AND SEE

Jesus...said to them, "What are you looking for?" They said to him, "Rabbi" (which translated means Teacher), "where are you staying?" He said to them, "Come, and you will see."

John 1:38-39

When I turn to Jesus in prayer, seeking consolation or perhaps guidance in making a critical decision, I hear him ask me, "What are you seeking?" Often, I don't know because my heart is filled with grief or my thoughts continually race toward the worst-case scenario. It's tempting to look for cheap hope in what the world offers as a distraction from our pain. Jesus alone knows what I need in these difficult times. In the stillness of prayer, I hear Jesus invite me with the same words he spoke to the first disciples: "Come, and you will see."

Jesus, Shelter of Hope, your presence is enough to console me and give me peace.

Deborah A. Meister

RELYING ON FAITH

Do not let your hearts be troubled. You have faith in God; have faith also in me. John 14:1

Early in my work as a hospital chaplain, when I received my daily patient lists along with meetings I had to attend, I would often panic. My boss would say, "Jim, stay calm. Concentrate on each person you speak to: listen to what you hear yourself say and what they say. You will find time for everything."

That, I believe, is Jesus' teaching here: Do not *let* your heart be—or *stay*—troubled. Have faith in God and in him. Yet each troubling moment makes me want to panic again—like parents desperate to help their teens but unable to find a way; or a soldier and family separated, deeply missing and fearful for one another; or anyone caught in economic troubles.

We have good and sane reasons to be troubled because there are so many troubles everywhere. Even Jesus had such troubles, but he didn't dwell on them. In speaking these words at his Last Supper, with his death inevitable and soon, Jesus spoke and heard his own faith in his Father. And he offered that same faith to his followers.

Fr. James Krings

Equal Opportunity Healing

Jesus said to the centurion, "You may go; as you have believed, let it be done for you." And at that very hour [his] servant was healed. Matthew 8:13

Let's face it. For many of us, one-to-one ministry may come most easily when we're helping people who are like us: our families or friends or neighbors. It's more difficult when we attempt to reach out to those who don't share our faith or political views or cultural background.

But there shouldn't be a difference. Jesus didn't turn away the centurion's plea for a paralyzed servant because the men were Gentiles. And he healed Peter's mother-in-law even though her being a woman made her a second-class citizen at that time in history.

There are qualities of Christ in all we serve: the young woman at an abortion clinic, the mentally ill and homeless man at the food pantry, the recent immigrant who needs help furnishing her family's apartment. When we fail to recognize that, we fail him.

Jesus, let me see you in everyone.

Melanie Rigney

Giving to God All That Cripples Us

> ...she was bent over, completely incapable of standing erect.
>
> Luke 13:11

This is a Gospel passage I can understand because it is about me. Perhaps it's about you too. This badly stooped woman has no name, so she can represent any of us. Let's meditate today on the things that sap our strength. What cripples us, causing us to bend over with burdens too heavy to bear?

The spirit that drains our strength has many names and faces. We've probably encountered all of these at one time or another: resentments crowd out forgiveness, fear smothers our love, indifference stifles our passion, suspicion dampens our trust, selfishness inhibits our generosity, busyness steals time from our prayer, jealousy dims our hospitality, greed stunts our gratitude, anxiety enshrouds our joy.

These are heavy burdens we ought not have to bear. They bend us to the breaking point. Let us find hope in the healing hands of Jesus as we behold this crippled woman standing up straight and giving glory to God. We can hand over to God all those things that cripple us. Come, let us walk into those healing hands and let them hold us.

Sr. Macrina Wiederkehr, O.S.B.

Trusting in the Presence

At once Jesus spoke to them, "Take courage, it is I; do not be afraid." Matthew 14:27

After Jesus has spent himself ministering to a crowd, he climbs up a mountain seeking some quiet, restorative time to pray and be alone in stillness. When evening arrives and darkness falls, he returns to find his disciples terrified as their boat is battered by violent wind and huge waves. Jesus takes in the scene, walks across the wild sea and utters the words repeated so often in Scripture, "Don't be afraid."

Easier said than done, we might say. The winds didn't immediately relent and die down. The waves continued to crash against the side of the boat. What made the difference is that the disciples were no longer alone, for Jesus was with them. When our own lives are battered by crises or threatened by anxiety, anguish, loss, may we center ourselves in stillness and prayer and remember that Jesus is also and always present with us.

Sr. Chris Koellhoffer, I.H.M.

ROOTED IN REALITY

**Our help is in the name of the LORD,
who made heaven and earth.** Psalm 124:8

When the computer makes a strange noise and the screen goes dark, I may be profoundly distressed, but I know where to go for help. The same is true if a little light flashes on the dashboard, the newspaper fails to arrive on time or part of the roof blows off in a storm. Such problems can be fixed. Help can be had.

But what if the doctor tells me an unusual spot has appeared on the x-ray of my lung? Or I discover I have been betrayed by a dear and trusted friend? Or that my child has been injured in a terrible car accident? If such things were to happen, where's the help?

Faith in God is often caricatured as an escape from reality, a fantasy of wishful thinking. But in my most trying moments, I have been able to immerse myself in reality only by finding help in God and in those who came in God's name.

In the hope that the conviction of this psalm verse will be with me when I need it most, I like to repeat it to myself from time to time. That way, I can be rooted in the reality of heaven and earth.

Mark Neilsen

Hope in Changing Seasons

**And you shall be secure, because there is hope;
you shall look round you and lie down in safety.** Job 11:18

In the many years I have lived in America, I have become acutely aware of the beauty of the changing seasons and the lessons embedded in them. During this time of year, I notice how the colors of the leaves change, just as our lives change with time. The leaves also fall to the ground as if they are prepared to fall asleep in the arms of their Creator, knowing they will be born again as nourishing topsoil.

Our lives change—people come and go, our hair turns gray, our plans evolve. But can we embrace the lesson of the falling leaves? Do we have the hopeful expectation of being transformed by God's love? Where may we find hope in the changing seasons of our lives?

Everliving God, help us be transformed through our hope in you.

Vivian Amu

What God Uses for His Glory

I will rather boast most gladly of my weaknesses, in order that the power of Christ may dwell with me. 2 Corinthians 12:9

There's a squirrel that's been hopping around our house for a while. He caught my eye because he only has a stump of a tail. This clearly makes a difference in his movement. His jumps are shorter, less like floating, and he lands more forcefully on the ground. He's not nearly as graceful as his kin.

The squirrel doesn't know how his movement is impacted by this limitation. I have countless limitations too, or thorns in the flesh, as Paul describes his own. I know about of some of these weaknesses, and others I probably bear like the squirrel with the stumpy tail, unaware of how they impact me.

The squirrel has adapted. I can too, but I can do even more. I can give the broken, stumpy parts of me—hidden or known that seem to keep me close to the ground—and let God use them, trusting that he will, for his glory.

Amy Welborn

No Small Matters

His master said to him, "Well done, my good and faithful servant. Since you were faithful in small matters, I will give you great responsibilities. Come, share your master's joy."

Matthew 25:21

All good gifts have their provenance in God. The Parable of the Talents (Matthew 25:14-30) exhorts us to make good use of all that God gives us.

What's more, when it comes to God, there are no small matters. God sees and knows everything about us—and the day we take hold of that truth will be a great grace for us. For then we will not ignore or overlook what, to others, may seem trivial, or less than, or irrelevant...keeping the faith even in small matters.

We are precious to the heart of God, and we can have great hope that we will be rewarded for our good stewardship of what is placed within our care. Using our gifts both humbly and honorable is the path to joy.

Lord, in the midst of my day-to-day challenges, help me to find new ways to be a good steward—in gratitude for all you have given to me.

Pat Gohn

Faith in the Unfaithful

If we are unfaithful
he remains faithful,
for he cannot deny himself. 2 Timothy 2:13

I learned an important lesson as a young boy: Be true to your friends and they will be true to you. The many friends I have made and kept over the years are a testament to this idea of mutual respect and trust.

But it took much longer—maybe a lifetime of both failures and successes—to learn that God plays by different rules. God is not faithful because we are. God does not wait for us to be faithful before acting in our lives. God does not love because we love. God loves first and strongest because God *is* undeniable and unrelenting love. Even in the face of our weaknesses and reluctance, and, even when we deny and betray and shove God aside to make room for something else, God remains faithful. In that simple but unfathomable truth is all the hope we need.

I hope in your faithful presence and love, my God.

Steve Givens

Forgetting and Remembering

...take care not to forget the Lord... Deuteronomy 6:12

It's the arc of life. You hear your elders complaining about forgetting things, and then it's your turn. With increasing frequency these days, I kick myself for leaving out a connecting thought in a homily or in a talk to the community. I tell myself it's best not to obsess, that God will take care of it. But that, too, is a work in progress.

What matters is not to forget the important things. At the time of covenant renewal, the people of Israel are reminded of all the goods of the promised land that are theirs, but only as gifts of God. We know what this is like. The more consumed we become by our own activities and by the stuff that fills our lives, the greater the risk of our forgetting the Source of everything truly good.

Maybe this is the silver lining in the forgetfulness of advancing years: to be grateful for what really matters and to stop sweating all the other stuff.

Fr. Dennis Gallagher, A.A.

Autumn Leaves

Faith is the realization of what is hoped for and evidence of things not seen. Hebrews 11:1

November will soon be here. It is my mother's month. She was born into it and, coming full circle, she passed beyond it. Autumn is achingly beautiful—transient with color, and so was she—this layered woman of spirit. But her memories abandoned her one by one. As she turned inward, I prayed for something—anything—we could share together. And God provided.

On technicolor Sundays, when leaves dropped like confetti, the two of us would go for brief rides to catch the fall colors in the sunlight. I would drive and she would point out all the bushes turning fiery red. Her fascination with them delighted her and became a gift for me. I had never, ever really noticed any of them before.

Every November, my eyes continue to be drawn to those remarkable burning bushes she loved. I see her in them all. And I am grateful.

Help us, Lord, to trust you in all the seasons of our lives.

Gail Goleas

How to Love One Another

Beloved, if God so loved us, we also must love one another.

1 John 4:11

Jesus commands us to love one another. We are called to love people, even people who are different from us in any number of ways. Love compels me to be kind and nonjudgmental to all people. But when I try to live this Jesus-inspired love of others, I encounter problems because some people think, speak and act in ways that are very inappropriate. Sadly, within society, there are individuals who may be vicious criminals. Even though they are in the minority, these people are included in the worldwide population in which I am to love one another. What should we do? What would Jesus do? Better yet, let us remember what Jesus already did—and still does. He hated sinful conduct and strongly condemned it. And yet, he always gives another chance, for us and others, to reform. When we can hope for and pray for weak and misguided human beings, we then are offering love to one another.

Fr. James McKarns

Brokenhearted But Okay

**The Lord is close to the brokenhearted;
and those who are crushed in spirit he saves.** Psalm 34:19

I have never felt God's power and presence as profoundly in ordinary times as I have in my weakest moments. When life is going along okay, I can be lulled into thinking that "I've got this." My ego leads me into the lie that I am self-sufficient, smart and capable apart from God. That's the key. I actually am sufficient, smart and capable. But apart from God, I can do nothing. He is my source for everything. This is why, when life pulls the rug out from under me and suddenly I am hopeless and helpless, I feel his mighty hand reach down to pull me up and guide me. In these moments, I know beyond knowing that I've got nothing. It doesn't terrify me to recognize this—it comforts me. It takes my breath away to even recall these times. If you are brokenhearted or your spirit is crushed, or you love someone who is in this place, know this: God is close. He sees. He is already saving. It's going to be okay.

Kristin Armstrong

ALLOWING OURSELVES TO FEEL

Harden not your hearts... Hebrews 3:8

The injunction, "harden not your hearts," is a frequent one in Scripture. It reminds us that God wants our hearts to be soft and sensitive to the movements of the Spirit and to the needs of others. How do we keep our hearts pliable?

First, we have to stay in touch with our own brokenness and pain. Mindful of our own wounds, we will be more apt to reach out to bind the wounds of others. Second, we must become more aware of individuals who need our help. We can offer to drive someone to the store or doctor, rent a documentary on human trafficking, serve at a homeless shelter, attend a talk on world hunger or babysit for busy parents. And third, we can do what you are doing right now: take a few minutes each day to reflect on the Scriptures, to focus on our faith and to ask God for help.

The American poet Archibald MacLeish wrote many years ago, "the great crime against life is not to feel." Allow yourself to feel today and every day.

Sr. Melannie Svoboda, S.N.D.

Reaching Out

I am concerned about you and about the way you are being treated in Egypt. Exodus 3:16

When we are feeling low, frightened or discouraged, is there any sweeter balm than a friend or a spouse expressing concern and a willingness to comfort us? Just the expression of concern can be enough to ease our pain. What we don't always realize is that when someone reaches out to us, it may be the literal answer to our prayer.

The Lord heard the sufferings of his people enslaved in Egypt. His emissary was Moses, sent to tell the people that the Lord cared about them and how they were being treated. Their prayers had been heard. True to his covenant with his chosen people, God would send Moses to lead his people to "a land flowing with milk and honey."

Often, the Lord's emissary in our own lives is that concerned friend who reaches out. Sometimes it is us who are asked to reach out to others.

Jesus, help me to be generous when I am called to ease someone else's burden.

Greg Erlandson

Share Your Hope Today

But when these signs begin to happen, stand erect and raise your heads because your redemption is at hand. Luke 21:28

We know that this world will eventually end. The sun will burn out and the world will go cold. More to the point, each of our lives will end much sooner. If we were a people without faith, the prospect of this world's destruction, and the destruction of our own lives, could be terrifying. We might be overcome with despair. As the world slides into secularism, this could be increasingly true for many. But the Scriptures tell us Christians to "stand erect and raise your heads" because our "redemption is at hand." Facing the end, or even amid the daily trials of life, we are a people of hope. Perhaps, today, you could share your hope with one other person. You could tell of the new heavens and the new earth that are coming. You could speak of the new life that we have found in Jesus.

Msgr. Stephen J. Rossetti

Join the Cloud of Witnesses

And he gave some as apostles, others as prophets, others as evangelists, others as pastors and teachers, to equip the holy ones for the work of ministry, for building up the body of Christ... Ephesians 4:11-12

We hear the stories of the martyrs, of the Church's great writers, of missionaries...and we wonder how we can possibly hope to feed on the scraps from their plates, much less eat with them at the heavenly table! We tell ourselves we're not that good...not that holy.

Ah, but that is evil whispering in our ears. Heaven is full of canonized and uncanonized wives, husbands, mothers, fathers, sisters, brothers—people no one outside their families and friends ever knew—all of whom hope and pray for us to join them. Like us, they struggled with pride, anxiety and temptation on earth. Like them, each of us has a special place in God's plan. Trust and hope—and their inspiration—help steady us on our path to join the cloud of witnesses.

All you holy people of God, please pray for me to walk with hope today.

Melanie Rigney

Hope in a World of Hurt

...so that you may not grieve like the rest, who have no hope.

1 Thessalonians 4:13

St. Paul's letter not only talks about our grieving for our beloved dead, but the necessity of grounding our grief in the hope of the resurrection.

November is the month our Church invites us to pray for departed souls. This timely season of praying for souls relies on the truth of Jesus' resurrection and the promise of his coming again. And while we know "neither the day nor the hour" (Matthew 25:13) of his coming, we look to Christ who suffered and died for us—and rose again.

Jesus is our true hope in this world and in the next. This month-long hope-filled prayer of the Church is a powerful consolation. Let us join our prayers to it with vigor.

Lord, have mercy on all those who have died, especially those names I bring to you now.

Pat Gohn

Faithful Companion

[Jesus] went up the mountain and summoned those whom he wanted and they came to him. Mark 3:13

Jesus chose twelve men to be his companions. They embodied many all-too-human traits. As time passed, they would reveal by their words and actions impatience, fear, betrayal, doubt, misunderstanding, impetuousness, pettiness. These would be balanced by courage, steadfastness, faithfulness, trust, goodness, purity of heart. All in all, these companions housed many of the same traits that both plague and delight us, for we can easily find them within ourselves. Despite their shortcomings, Jesus remained faithful to them. Jesus loved them, encouraged them, forgave them and trusted them. He gave them a share in his own spirit. We share in that gift as well and are called to be patient with each other in this journey of life. Great and powerful mysteries came forth from these companions of Jesus, though they barely grasped the import of them. We are living vessels of God's grace and power, even in our weakest moments.

Fr. James Stephen Behrens, O.C.S.O.

Fanning the Flames

For this reason, I remind you to stir into flame the gift of God that you have through the imposition of my hands. For God did not give us a spirit of cowardice but rather of power and love and self-control. 2 Timothy 1:6-7

For our wedding anniversary last year, my wife and I treated ourselves to a new firepit that is designed to recirculate oxygen, creating a dancing fire and very little smoke. It was a particular blessing for patio gatherings in the pandemic era, when our understandable anxieties kept us from enjoying our normal social and family activities.

Paul reminds the timid Timothy that God has begun a magnificent work in him. The Holy Spirit is already bearing fruit in his life and ministry. Yet it's not a passive operation. Grace requires some cooperation from us, inviting a response to the free gift that Jesus offers.

How will I use today to poke at the coals, blow on the embers and stir into flame the faith, hope and love that God has poured into my heart?

Steve Pable

November 4

Beside Us Always

**Indeed he neither slumbers nor sleeps,
the guardian of Israel.** Psalm 121:4

When we love someone, we keep vigil. We resist sleep and wait up until we hear our teenager's car pull into the driveway safely. We sit in reverent presence by the bedside of a family member approaching her last hours among us. We accompany a friend to a doctor's office when the diagnosis he might hear is uncertain. We share the excited anticipation of a neighbor awaiting news of a hoped-for job. In our own loving and limited way, we reveal what the psalmist observes of the Holy One—that at every moment of our lives, our God remains with us as a loving presence. Our God guards our coming and our going in the ways of peace.

Sr. Chris Koellhoffer, I.H.M.

'Not a Museum for Saints'

This man welcomes sinners and eats with them. Luke 15:2

Abigail Van Buren once wrote that, "a church is a hospital for sinners, not a museum for saints." I love museums. They are one of the first places I seek out when I visit a new city. But if—as some people would lead us to believe—our Church is nothing more than a collection of historical exhibits and dusty books, we are worshipping in vain. "Dear Abby" got it right.

As important as history and tradition is to our Church, our faith is not a museum exhibit filled with long-dead specimens, stuffed and propped up to show us what the "real thing" looks like. Our Church is and must be alive and real, and that means it is filled with fragile, weak, sinful humans. Jesus welcomes us to his Church just as we are and invites us to dine with him at the eucharistic table. When we do, we come into real and pure communion with him and receive his mercy, healing and forgiveness. That's Church.

Jesus, welcome me into your healing presence.

Steve Givens

Take Grief to the Lord

...but a double portion to Hannah because he loved her, though the Lord had made her barren. 1 Samuel 1:5

Barrenness can be defined in many ways, not just the inability to have a child. Barrenness can mean brokenness, unfulfilled dreams, empty parts of your heart, dashed hopes, neglected passions, anything that hasn't turned out the way you'd planned. Like Hannah, we all grieve the areas of our life that aren't showing signs of growth.

The important thing about grief is to know where to take it: to God. He can handle the full weight of our grief, the total measure of our frustration and disappointment. Go ahead, vent. But in the wake of that expression of emotion, it is crucial to maintain an open, trusting heart. Barrenness is not always a permanent state for those who trust in the Lord; Hannah later had a son named Samuel.

Pour your heart out to the Lord and dedicate your future fulfillment to him. Have faith as each chapter of your story is written. Our God specializes in the impossible.

Kristin Armstrong

Imperfect

O stupid Galatians! Who has bewitched you...? Galatians 3:1

The disciples in Galatia had come under the influence of imposters, and Paul was angry, plain and simple. Can you blame him? He worked hard to help found their community of believers, after all, and they let themselves be led astray. When he got word about it, Paul didn't gently guide them back to the true faith. He let them have it! "Why are you listening to those people? What's the *matter* with you?!"

Was this holy anger? You bet. It was also undeniably human, and that fills me with hope. Like Paul, I am prone to anger, impatience and resentment. Yet Paul, saint and apostle, used those very qualities in service of the Gospel. If he could serve the Lord and spread the Good News despite his all-too-human tendencies, then maybe I can too.

Saint Paul, I am imperfect, but I long to serve the Lord. Please pray for me!

Karla Manternach

Keep Listening No Matter What

...there was a tiny whispering sound. When he heard this, Elijah hid his face in his cloak and went and stood at the entrance of the cave. 1 Kings 19:12-13

Elijah had walked 40 days and nights to reach God's mountain, Horeb. He sought shelter in that cave after experiencing terrible turmoil—prophets being put to death by the sword—and he barely escaped with his life! The Lord was passing by, and Elijah was waiting for him. There was violent wind, an earthquake and fire. But Elijah had a heart attentive and attuned to God. Even with all he had been through, and despite all the fantastic tumult around him, he listened for the still small voice.

Many of us may be reeling from the troubles and tribulations we face. Yet let us approach that holy place where we can hear God in prayer. Amid the chaos, may we keep listening for God, no matter what comes.

Do you have a special place where you pray? Do you schedule a regular appointment with God, a daily prayer time? If so, don't flag in your zeal, be sure to show up. God longs to meet you there.

Pat Gohn

In Praise of Heroes

As gold in the furnace, he proved them,
and as sacrificial offerings he took them to himself.

Wisdom 3:6

St. Leo the Great, whose feast we celebrate today, surely was tried in that furnace spoken of in this reading. Leo had to fight the barbarians and the heretics. He pleaded for his people and was finally responsible for turning back Attila the Hun, who would have destroyed Rome.

Besides all this, Leo was expected to minister to his people's spiritual and bodily needs. You might think such heroic things would never be asked of you, but think again. Is it not heroic to endure yet another surgery, make one more courteous phone call, help another shoulder a burden, avoid one more quarrel with a contentious customer and through all of this to keep your faith and trust in God alive? It is *how* we endure all these situations that determines who we become through them all. May we, like St. Leo, see Jesus taking us to himself and whispering encouraging words to us.

Please, God, may this be so in this new day you are granting me.

Sr. Charleen Hug, S.N.D.

Journeying in Hope

And as for those who do not welcome you, when you leave that town, shake the dust from your feet in testimony against them. Luke 9:5

I went to a museum exhibit about World War I and the visual arts. Every display seemed to carry the same story of crushed ideals. The enthusiastic had stepped into the doings of war, enthralled and hopeful, but then stumbled away, dispirited, appalled and broken. I remember how I've lived this dynamic myself, albeit in less serious ways—as a classroom teacher, a parent, a person involved in trying to help others, perhaps even in terms of my own sense of self. How can we continue to hope in the face of harsh, unwelcoming reality? Who knows the answer better than Jesus? In him, I see and hear it: accept reality, respect others' freedom and discern the way forward strengthened by the love and grace that comes only from him.

Jesus, be with me on today's journey. As I meet limits and disappointment, may I still keep my eyes on you.

Amy Welborn

New Things are Coming

So whoever is in Christ is a new creation: the old things have passed away; behold, new things have come.

2 Corinthians 5:17

For much of my life, hope has been a struggle for me to grasp. It's not that it's the most difficult for me to *have*, but that it's the most challenging to describe or understand. At times, I know that I oversimplified hope—equating it with a positive attitude. I can see now that there's a temptation to cheapen the virtue of hope with papered-on optimism. Christian hope, though, isn't cheery denial. Salvation history and the Cross of Christ reminds us repeatedly what sort of struggles we're embracing. As members of the body of Christ, we believe in transformation. We change from the inside out, as we act for the fullness of God's love to be widely known. This interior and exterior conversion is only possible with God. We see new things coming as the old passes away. That's what hope is made of: knowing that there's newness after tough times.

Sr. Julia Walsh, F.S.P.A.

Restoring Divisions

So a division occurred in the crowd because of him. Some of them even wanted to arrest him, but no one laid hands on him. John 7:43-44

The crowd is having a hard time knowing what is true. Uncertainty brings about polarization, and conversations become difficult, even among friends and neighbors. Without even listening to one another, they condemn. When political events, say, disrupt our assumptions of basic agreement, tensions quickly emerge. The search for a scapegoat holds out the hope that by eliminating him, her or them, we will once again enjoy peace. In a way, Jesus was just such a scapegoat, though not as his opponents imagined. By his willing submission to the depths of human hostility, the innocent Lord loved us at our very worst. His dying and rising proved once and for all that destroying a scapegoat will not end violence. What, then, will end violence and restore community? The Cross provides an answer if we open our hearts to the love that is offered there.

Mark Neilsen

CLAIMING GOD'S LOVE

**Beside restful waters he leads me;
he refreshes my soul.** Psalm 23:2-3

At the funeral Mass of a beloved young man, we sang these words. This psalm, and all the readings and hymns, were chosen by his parents in consultation with the priest. The homily, too, spoke radiantly, forcefully, of God's overflowing mercy and care for his flock—spoken not lightly, but from the very depths, like Jonah from the belly of the whale. I am in awe that, in the darkest valley, those so deeply grieving could claim God's love so ringingly. Is it true that the resurrection is best glimpsed through tears, as Mary Magdalene saw it? Where could such faith and hope come from? Only love sees truly.

In sorrow and in joy, O Lord, you spread the table before me. You refresh my soul.

Mary Marrocco

Life Everlasting

So they set out at once and returned to Jerusalem where they found gathered together the eleven and those with them who were saying, "The Lord has truly been raised and has appeared to Simon!" Luke 24:33-34

Imagine the pain that gripped the hearts of Jesus's followers during the time of his passion and death. Imagine the transformation that occurred in their hearts when they heard that he was risen. After the initial shock, they were filled with incredible joy. The promise of Jesus that he would always be with them came true, and it was a promise that included us too!

What happened to Jesus will also happen to us. We are all destined to pass through death to resurrected life because God wants our relationship with him to be without end. What depths of love! That is how important we are to God!

Jesus our hope, your loving presence rests in the heart of every person. May we find our unity with one another in the sharing of that love.

Fr. Kenneth E. Grabner, C.S.C.

Hopeful Even On My Down Days

**Even there your hand shall guide me,
and your right hand hold me fast.** Psalm 139:10

"Even there," when I am sick, when I am in dread of what comes next, when I think of wars and the worst misfortunes, even there, O God who made light and darkness as one, who scatters the darkness of sin, you hold me fast.

How could the mighty God be as approachable to me as a father or mother? How can darkness and light be one? When can I stop deciding I have all the answers, that I know the mind of God? Even there, your hand holds me fast. I want to believe that with all my heart and soul. I want to believe that "even there" includes joys and sorrows, that I will feel you holding me up, perhaps through some compassionate person today. It's hard on a down day, but help me try to be compassionate for one person, too.

O You who know me so well, continue to hold me fast. I thank you even though I don't always feel your presence. Even there.

Sr. Marguerite Zralek, O.P.

November 16

God's Enduring Love

**Give thanks to the Lord, for he is good,
for his mercy endures forever.** Psalm 118:1

Almost daily I am reminded that everything is transitory. Yesterday's world leaders are dying off, celebrated sports figures from my youth are now dealing with debilitating illnesses, and once fresh-faced celebrities are entering their senior years. Nothing in this world is permanent, and life continues to remind us of that truth. All of this would be depressing if it were not for our faith in a God who is love. If we allow that love to grow in us, our lives will continue to have meaning and purpose no matter what is happening to our bodies. Anyone who has sincerely tried to love without restrictions knows that this is a never-ending challenge and not for the faint of heart. However, even in the midst of turmoil, we can live with a sense of hope that no matter what befalls us, God's enduring love will have the final word.

Terri Mifek

Is This Possible?

Rejoice always. 1 Thessalonians 5:16

Some explanation may help to relieve the seeming impossibility of this command. "Rejoice" here does not mean "feel happy," but "find your source of joy and express your thanks." We can certainly always remind ourselves of God's love and of our hope of being with him forever. But can we always really find joy in that? In some situations—I am thinking of my daughter whose own daughter is sick—to rejoice seems beyond human ability, even contrary to human nature. Perhaps it is significant that the Greek translation here is plural, directed to a group. "You all, rejoice always." Paul speaks of rejoicing in God's love, in hope, as something we do *together*. Perhaps he envisions us accompanying each other in our struggles, helping one another, bearing one another's burdens, so that those who have sorrow are carried along by being part of a community that rejoices and hopes in the Lord. In that case, rejoicing always is something we do by reaching out to one another. Paradoxically, rejoicing may involve weeping with those who weep, as Paul also says in Romans 12:15.

Kevin Perrotta

Being a Pesky Widow

...pray always without becoming weary. Luke 18:1

This story about the unjust judge holds a certain charm. (See Luke 18:1-8.) I am not exactly likening God to the unjust judge. Yet if persistent requests gain attention from someone who isn't all that interested in the person who is in need, what might we expect when we ask a favor of someone who really cares? And that, of course, includes God. If we pray always, it means that we have learned to live awake to the truth that attentive living can, in itself, be a prayer. Attentive living guards us against asking for inappropriate favors. Not growing weary awakens us to the truth that we must learn to wait in hope. The ability to wait in hope rises out of a fierce trust in the goodness of God. I encourage you to become the pesky widow in your prayer requests to the Beloved. Keep asking for favors that are needed. Imagine your need, then lean into that image and do not lose heart. Wait with hope.

Sr. Macrina Wiederkehr, O.S.B.

LET THE SPIRIT DO THE HEALING

**For you will surely have a future,
and your hope will not be cut off.** Proverbs 23:18

As a seasoned spiritual director, I sometimes journey with individuals who feel undeserving of God's love. Their past sins, life experiences or present challenges cause them to think that God isn't listening or surely doesn't care about them. Our sessions are replete with their stories of childhood wounds, broken relationships and experiences of loss.

After each session I pray, returning their anguish and grief to God, lest I myself stagger under the burden. Sometimes I wonder if our sessions are helping anything or if I am the right companion. I can only make space for the Spirit to do the healing. I cannot fix their past or their perception of it. But I believe in healing, in God's steadfast love for each of them. I believe in their hopeful future, and so, if they desire, we make the next appointment.

Lord, help me to never give up hope for myself or for others.

Jennifer Christ

NOVEMBER 20

The Gifts of the Holy Spirit

While claiming to be wise, they became fools. Romans 1:22

This verse reminds me of the gifts of the Holy Spirit conferred on us in the Sacrament of Confirmation. Among the Spirit's gifts, wisdom, knowledge and understanding are given freely to us all. But despite this generous endowment, we still manage to say and do things that we often regret—hurtful things said in haste, boasting or bragging when we should be quiet, avoiding rash judgment.

These gifts bring us closer to God, closer to our faith as we strive to lead lives as followers of Christ. I can't imagine how many times I was saved from saying something foolish. But still many times I manage to open my mouth and let loose with a stupid comment or thought. It is at this time when another gift of the Holy Spirit hopefully kicks in: counsel or right judgment, when we know the difference between right and wrong, and we choose to do what is right. Sometimes what is right is not saying anything.

Holy Spirit, thank you for your gifts. Make them a part of all I say and do.

Paul Pennick

Christ, Our King!

Say among the nations: The Lord is king. Psalm 96:10

The first parish where I served as pastor was Christ Our King. I still recall those lovely parishioners and the many events we shared over ten years. Our feast day was the last Sunday of the liturgical year when we honor Christ as King. People from outside the parish would often refer to the church as Christ the King. "No," we would say, "it's Our King." We liked the possessive adjective in the name for it was a reminder that we should have a close relationship to Christ. Among the many titles of Jesus, that of king is very fitting since it ideally designates one who is in charge and cares for people with trust and responsibility. It is often mentioned that the United States does not have a king. However, something that gives me great hope for the future is that one of our most patriotic songs, America the Beautiful, asks our God to "shed his grace" on upon our country.

Lord of nations, enlighten and strengthen our minds and hearts.

Fr. James McKarns

November 22

GOD'S 'INSTIGATING LOVE'

God so loved the world... John 3:16

These five words from the Gospel remind us that everything proceeds from God's love—*everything*! The universe itself was loved into being by God, and it continues to exist and unfold because of God's love. Salvation, too, proceeds from love—the love of the Trinity: Father, Son and Spirit. As children of God, we are privileged to share in that dynamic trinitarian love.

Sometimes our faith can get too negative or shortsighted. This happens when we focus on what's wrong with everything (including ourselves) or on who's right and who's wrong, who's in and who's out. Instead of formulating rigid distinctions, our faith should first and foremost fill us with awe before the marvelous mystery and diversity of existence. It should fill our hearts with gratitude for God's incredible "instigating love." Everything begins with that love.

Sr. Melannie Svoboda, S.N.D.

Courage to Witness to the Faith

This is how he died, leaving in his death a model of courage and an unforgettable example of virtue not only for the young but for the whole nation. 2 Maccabees 6:31

Being an example is an important part of our Catholic faith. I feel that especially keenly in the Appalachian region where I live. Catholics are a tiny minority, and it takes courage to claim the faith.

Through my work, especially in this poverty-plagued region, I've witnessed Catholics whose lives of courage and virtue compel them to reach out to those in need. Volunteers work with children, hoping to assist them in finding a better life than those who came before them. Others visit the elderly, repair homes, stock food pantries and comfort the abused. These people of conviction share their faith through a powerful example of selfless service, evangelizing their entire community in the process. And although I see powerful examples here, I know they are at work throughout the world.

Dear Lord, please give us the courage to provide example in our daily actions.

Beth Dotson Brown

Recalling What God Has Done

Hear now, all you who fear God, while I declare what he has done for me. Psalm 66:16

In my weakest moments, when fear threatens to engulf me and my unbelief taunts me, I recall how God has saved me in the past.

I have a list of these intimate miracles—when God has gone before me and turned an impossible situation around, when circumstances were so aligned against me that the presence of an Almighty God was the only explanation remaining after the dust settled. I recall when I had a hiding place in a storm, when my heart was gently placed on the other side of a cavern. He has prevailed on my behalf; he has never abandoned or forsaken me in my need, no matter how unworthy I felt at the time. When I speak these memories out loud, something shifts. The heavens open in response to my praise, and my heart opens in response to his power.

Kristin Armstrong

God's Plan for Us

They can no longer die, for they are like angels; and they are the children of God because they are the ones who will rise.

Luke 20:36

As I look at my life, I find so many reasons to give thanks. It is important for me to remember the good things of life and to see them as God's blessings. But as good as this life has been, the best is yet to come. That is God's promise to all of us.

When this life ends, we graduate into a new way of being. We become more aware of God's tremendous love for us and more awake to the beauty of the universe God has made. Our awareness will fill us with tremendous love and joy. Sorrows, along with disappointments and failures, will be things of the past. This is God's ultimate plan for us.

Lord, when it is time for me to let go of this life, may I not be afraid. Instead, may I be filled with hope in your promises and with anticipation of sharing fully in your joy.

Fr. Kenneth E. Grabner, C.S.C.

A Mission From the King

> Then the king will say to those on his right, "Come, you who are blessed by my Father. Inherit the kingdom prepared for you from the foundation of the world. For I was hungry and you gave me food, I was thirsty and you gave me drink, a stranger and you welcomed me, naked and you clothed me, ill and you cared for me, in prison and you visited me."
>
> Matthew 25:34-36

In Baptism we not only possess a precious identity and dignity as beloved sons and daughters of God, but a promised inheritance. This Gospel reminds us that at the Second Coming, no one will mistake Jesus Christ as our king. Those who have followed Jesus and his ways—performing the works of mercy he recommends—will inherit this Kingdom, to the delight of our heavenly Father. *That* is our promised future glory.

But in the meantime, we still have a mission from the king. The Kingdom we seek is found in our knowledge as blessed sons and daughters of God and in our living faith—by seeing and serving the sacred dignity of others. For when we serve others, we serve Christ.

Lord Jesus, strengthen me to serve with love every day.

Pat Gohn

LOOKING FORWARD

God is faithful... 1 Corinthians 1:9

The holy season of Advent is another time of resolutions. The ones we made in January have perhaps fizzled out or have even been forgotten. Perhaps, with reflection, we may be asking ourselves, *what was I thinking?* In making new resolutions, we may have decided that we will put a hush in the rush of Advent and not succumb to the hustle and bustle of Christmas.

Make no mistake. Advent resolutions are good and do give us a focus. But we likely realize that they will give way to the demands of Christmas preparations—sending cards, baking cookies, shopping and wrapping presents.

Advent is not a time for discouragement or pious thoughts of our expected fidelity. God alone is faithful. God asks that, each day, we begin again. Perhaps this is the true message of Advent. Both Mary and Joseph had to lean on God. With their careful plans shattered, they began again. They did not look back, only forward, leaning on the absolute belief in God's faithfulness. Can we do the same?

Sr. Bridget Haase, O.S.U.

DANCING WITH ANGELS

He redeems your life from destruction,
he crowns you with kindness and compassion…

Psalm 103:4

Strange that Jesus says his yoke is easy and his burden light (Matthew 11:30). Did he not take on the misery, suffering and sin of the whole human race? Don't we see, daily and nightly, what a huge, seemingly relentless burden this is?

He not only took them on, he went deeper into them than we could ever know. Imagine the darkest pit you have ever fallen into, the most vile and oppressive human situation you have ever known of—and the past century has made it hard for us not to see such things. Such things are around us and within us also. This is exactly the place where God most surely comes to meet us, to redeem us from the pit. What does he bring there? Mercy and compassion. Our burdens, sins and sufferings are heavy enough to crush us; God's mercy and compassion are light and airy and make us dance with the angels. Why carry anything else?

Bless the Lord, my soul; dance with mercy and sing with compassion, which the Lord has poured forth.

Mary Marrocco

HOPE EMERGING OUT OF SUFFERING

Here is a true Israelite. There is no duplicity in him. John 1:47

I cannot approach this day, the feast of St. Andrew, without thinking of my beloved nephew, who was not only named Andrew, his birthday is this week. He died tragically in a car accident some years ago, but his memory is fresh in our minds. Such never really fade.

For our family, the pain and sense of loss were almost beyond bearing. Yet there was at the time, and it persists to this day, a sense of Andrew's kindness and goodness. We feel a consolation in recalling him and seeing his face in our minds.

I would never consider using the word "grace" to describe what happened. But we are graced with his life and still with his spirit that remains with us. Hope is not truly a Christian virtue without recognizing that it emerges out of human suffering.

There are many signs of hope in my life. Andrew's face is one of the most enduring.

Msgr. Stephen J. Rossetti

Upended Expectations

But she was greatly troubled at what was said and pondered what sort of greeting this might be. Then the angel said to her, "Do not be afraid, Mary, for you have found favor with God." Luke 1:29-30

As Christmas approaches, many of us are preparing for visitors. Or we are embarking on a visit ourselves. Kids are coming home from college; we're off to see our parents or friends. We know we'll be seeing friends or coworkers at events. It's something we expect with excitement, dread or indefinable emotions. We know what's coming. But do we?

We approach this season of encounters and visiting with expectations, as we do, really, every day in terms of our ordinary interactions. But, looking back, we can see how many times we've been surprised—expectations upended. We can expect all we want, but only God knows what these encounters hold. And so, with Mary, we move forward. We've heard who's coming, we open our doors, and we wait, trusting God, willing to be surprised.

O Lord, unlock the door of my heart that I may welcome your presence in every encounter.

Amy Welborn

HOPE AND TRUST

"...and they shall name him Emmanuel,"
which means "God is with us." Matthew 1:23

I recently heard that the two main motivations that influence human behavior are hopes for improved safety and quality of life. As I listened, it occurred to me to wonder whether these basic desires truly reflect gospel values. Invitations to discipleship often call us to reject safety and security. We are called to trust, abandon our possessions and love fearlessly. In this Advent season, we are invited to widen our hearts and deepen our hope and trust. We know that God's light shines brightly in the dark. We know that love is a stronger force than danger. May this understanding lodge deep in our hearts where we can reflect on it and allow it to shape our behavior. The messages to Joseph remain true for us all: "Do not be afraid" (Matthew 1:20) and "God is with us."

God, may my trust and love for you, more than my fears or greed, direct my actions.

Sr. Julia Walsh, F.S.P.A.

Waiting for a Spark

**The light shines in the darkness,
and the darkness has not overcome it.** John 1:5

I once went spelunking in a limestone cave in rural Missouri. We entered the small entrance on our hands and knees, and once we got beyond a few turns, our guide asked us to turn off our flashlights. I never imagined anything so dark. I couldn't see my hands in front of my face, and I panicked. What if the lights didn't come back on? No doubt we would be lost forever.

As we enter into Advent, I can imagine a similar panic. What if the light of Christ had never been lit? What if the Incarnate Word of God had not sparked to life in a Bethlehem manger cave? How lost in darkness would we be?

But we have seen the light. We live in and through it. We crawl toward it on hands and knees and know its pull and presence. Darkness can never overcome that kind of light.

Christ, be my light and hope.

Steve Givens

Wishin' and a-Hopin'

For in hope we were saved. Romans 8:24

We wish for much in this world—for books and music and gadgets that are on our birthday and Christmas lists. For the money to eat and dress and live as we like. For healing of physical, spiritual and emotional damage in ourselves and those we love. Sometimes we get what we wish for; sometimes we don't. But we have a pretty clear picture of what life would look like with those earthly dreams having come true. Consider, by contrast, what we hope the glory of heaven will be. Seeing all our relatives and friends? Meeting the Lord face to face? Singing with the celestial choir? None of us, with the possible exception of a few who have had near-death experiences, has much of an idea of what lies beyond. But we have the hope of salvation and glory. Come to think of it, those are pretty awesome things to hope for. What more could we desire?

Lord, help me have a strong hope for salvation.

Melanie Rigney

SEEING BEYOND

Then the wolf shall be a guest of the lamb...
  the lion shall eat hay like the ox.
The baby shall play by the viper's den,
  and the child lay his hand on the adder's lair.
They shall not harm or destroy on all my holy mountain;
  for the earth shall be filled with knowledge of the LORD...

Isaiah 3:6, 7-9

We could easily be confounded by the contrasts in this reading from Isaiah. What a countercultural, upside-down world, with the wolf a guest of the lamb, the lion eating hay like an ox, the baby playing right next door to a poisonous snake's habitat. Does that holy mountain devoid of any harm or ruin sound too good to be true? Well, then, Isaiah suggests, we should sharpen our spiritual eyesight and look beyond appearances. This is not some cockeyed optimism but a summons to live in genuine hope. It's a call to act out of an unshakable conviction that sin and death will not have the final word, that an alternative worldview grounded in compassion, welcome and acceptance is possible. During these Advent days, may we see beyond the surface, cultivate divine vision and work with God's grace to hasten the coming of this longed-for, peaceable Kingdom.

Sr. Chris Koellhoffer, I.H.M.

Habit of Hope

Always be ready to give an explanation…a reason for your hope… 1 Peter 3:15

As a teenager, I remember crowds packing into Saint Joseph's little clapboard church. One day at Mass, sandwiched between strangers and a sea of heads, a blue and white habit several pews up caught my eye. Moments later, I knew I was meant to talk with the woman in that habit. The recessional sounded; throngs swarmed between us. I waited. I looked. But the religious sister had disappeared into the crowd. *Okay, Lord, maybe I wasn't supposed to talk with her.*

Suddenly, I heard a thick German accent. "My dear, I thought I lost you. I believe the Holy Spirit wants us to talk."

Over the next several decades, Sr. M. Deogratia would become my habit of hope. She, much like Saint Nicholas, whose feast day is today, compassionately and generously gave from her heart. Her prayers carried me through my teens. Prompted by the Holy Spirit, Sister often sent handwritten encouragement, prayer cards and little remembrances—just when I needed them most. I treasured them; I treasured her.

Thank you, Lord, for encouragers, like Sr. M. Deogratia, always ready to share the reason for their hope.

Kathleen Swartz McQuaig

God of Surprises

> **Thus the total number of generations from Abraham to David is fourteen generations.** Matthew 1:17

As part of my preparation for a trip to Europe, I did a little research into my ancestry. The further I dug, the more intrigued I became by the stories I never knew. My family history was peppered with everything from tragic accidental deaths to several women with religious vocations. Most surprising, I learned that as a young widower, my grandfather had adopted a little girl after her mother died unexpectedly. Twists and turns are part of salvation history as well. The genealogy of Jesus is filled with surprising people, unexpected hardships, scandal as well as generosity and great faith. Their stories remind us that God's promises are fulfilled but not always as we would have expected or through the people we would have guessed. We wait in hope not because we know the future, but because we trust the God of surprises.

Terri Mifek

On Our Own

Then the angel departed from her. Luke 1:38

Mary performed her day-to-day household tasks with no clue as to how her story would end. Her "yes" did not bring a spoiler alert from the angel as to what she might expect in becoming the Mother of God.

Imagine the questions in the hearts of her parents, Ann and Joachim, devout Jews, on hearing that an angel came to their young daughter, asking her to be, through the overshadowing of the Holy Spirit, the mother of the Messiah. Their faith was stretched, but they believed.

After Mary's "yes," the angel departed from her. Except for her total reliance on God and her surrender to his message, she, like us, was on her own for the hard times ahead.

All of us receive messages—some that may seem impossible—from God. Our source of hope must be seared into our being—like Mary's—through our trust in the absolute fidelity of God, who renders all things well.

Mary, teach me to place my hope in our faithful God.

Sr. Bridget Haase, O.S.U.

A Path Out of Darkness

I came into the world as light, so that everyone who believes in me might not remain in darkness. John 12:46

The church at my parish has several mercury vapor lights. When there is a power outage, they go out like all the others. However, when the power returns, the mercury lights only gradually reach full brightness, compared to the other lights that go on immediately.

For me, these lights have come to symbolize one way the light of Christ shines in the world. I have been blessed personally, and I have seen Christ's brilliant light in others too. Then, like a finger snap, there is the darkness of personal illness, tragic loss, crushing evil. The darkness descends like a spiritual power outage that cannot be restored by any quick fix.

Instead, like a mercury vapor light, faith sparks again and grows gradually, the light of Christ leading us, in time, out of the darkness.

Dear Jesus, if I feel darkness today, shine your light in the crevices of my soul where I most need you.

Fr. James Kring

He Carried Me

> **...and he will continue to rescue us; in him we have put our hope that he will also rescue us again...** 2 Corinthians 1:10

I am fifty years old, so I have no idea why trials can still take me by surprise, but they do. Even if I know that God uses seasons of challenge to refine and strengthen us, I still react—at least initially—with some fear. I mistakenly measure myself against the challenge ahead and slip into old habits of worry or control. Until I remember.

It isn't my power that gets me to the other side. It's God's.

When I am afraid, the fastest path back to peace and courage is gratitude. I start thanking God—in my head, out loud, in my journal—and I recount all the times in the past where he has rescued me. I recall the feelings of awe as he solved something in a way I had never considered, or he removed a situation entirely. Every time he carried me. Every time he protected the people I love. Every time he tenderly put my heart back together.

Lord, thank you that you saved me then, and you are saving me now.

Kristin Armstrong

COMFORT AFTER SUFFERING

**Comfort, give comfort to my people,
says your God.** Isaiah 40:1

The experience of suffering is universal. Every one of us has had our lives disrupted by sickness, accident, loss of a loved one, etc. The prophet Isaiah references a group of Israelites that have been exiled to the pagan land of Babylon for nearly 70 years. But the new king of Babylon has decreed that they can return to their homeland. He will even send supplies and workers to help the Israelites rebuild their shattered city of Jerusalem. Isaiah is convinced that this is nothing less than the work of God. Every one of us can identify with this song of deliverance, whether it be recovery of health after an illness or a new job after the loss of a former one. Maybe it's the birth of a healthy child after a grim prognosis had been made. God brings comfort, hope and new life to a hurting people. The Church invites us during Advent to reflect on our experiences of God's comfort and to pray for an end to violence and oppression in our world.

Fr. Martin Pable, O.F.M. Cap.

THE LOVING GAZE OF MOTHER MARY

Sing and rejoice, O daughter Zion! See, I am coming to dwell among you, says the LORD. Many nations shall join themselves to the LORD on that day, and they shall be his people...

Zechariah 2:14-15

At Mass in a cathedral in Mexico one Sunday, we were seated near a large reproduction of Our Lady of Guadalupe. All through Mass, people came and knelt in front of the image, prayed and then returned to the congregation. One man knelt facing the altar on the cool stone floor in front of the image. Shabbily dressed, he rose from his knees only once, then winced, sat down and rolled up his trouser leg to reveal a terribly swollen calf. He rubbed it then returned to his knees, rocking back and forth, hands folded, lips moving continually in prayer, as Our Lady gazed down at him and he looked fervently at her. My heart filled, and I prayed for him, for the hope of the day, revealed in the loving gaze of the mother, when that man—and all of us—would sing and rejoice, whole and healthy, joyfully in the dwelling of the Lord.

Our Lady of Guadalupe, pray for us.

Amy Welborn

DECEMBER 12

An Unfailing Promise

I command you: be strong and steadfast! Do not fear nor be dismayed, for the Lord, your God, is with you wherever you go. Joshua 1:9

When the Israelites finally made their way into the Promised Land, it had been many generations since they'd had a place to call home. After their oppressive slavery in Egypt, they wandered, hard-hearted, in the wilderness for forty years. As they reached the Jordan, they looked with dread to all the other kingdoms who would oppose their entrance into Canaan. It's no wonder that Joshua, as leader of this uncertain nation, needed divine reassurance. In this promise to Joshua, we find a foreshadowing of Emmanuel, "God with us."

Here is the most consistent and compelling theme of salvation history: God does not abandon us. Rather, the Lord dwells among us, seeks us out, binds our wounds, strengthens our weak knees and restores us as beloved sons and daughters.

Lord, keep me steadfast in remembering your constant care and companionship!

Steve Pable

Hopeful Anticipation

For through the Spirit, by faith, we await the hope of righteousness. Galatians 5:5

I always find myself waiting for something. I am always waiting for a package in the mail, a phone call, a response to an email, payday or an answer to a prayer. I wait and hope, but sometimes I am restless. As I get older, I have found God waiting for me in my place of restlessness—and Advent reminds me to pay attention to my restlessness.

Advent is an invitation to fully enter into a state of hopeful anticipation for Christ's love, even in our restlessness. We might wonder how we are to sustain such faith and hope. There is no need to wonder. God has already given to us the loving gift of the Holy Spirit—sustaining us and giving us the courage we need to await all that is good—all that is for the glory of God.

Merciful God, help us remain faithful as we await all the good gifts you have for us.

Vivian Amu

December 14

A Real Eye-opener

> Then he touched their eyes and said, "Let it be done for you according to your faith." And their eyes were opened.
>
> Matthew 9:29-30

Having been blessed with good eyesight my whole life, it is tough for me to imagine how elated the two blind men from this Gospel story must have been upon being healed. They simply couldn't contain their joy. In fact, despite having been sternly warned by Jesus to not tell of their miraculous healing, they "went out and spread word of him [Jesus] through all that land" (verse 31).

Consider an instance when your eyes were opened, even if metaphorically, when you suddenly realized something with greater clarity. If it was a joyful revelation, I'm sure that you wanted to share this epiphany with others. Even if we have just a fraction of the faith that these blind men had, we should enthusiastically share it this Advent.

Jesus, Divine Healer, open my eyes and the eyes of my loved ones, friends and acquaintances. Help us to experience and share true Christmas joy this season.

Terence Hegarty

With a Sure Hope

Peace I leave with you... Do not let your hearts be troubled or afraid. John 14:27

For most of us, our Christmas preparations usually involve selecting gifts for our loved ones. We attempt to find a gift exactly right for each person: for Simon, a bird book; for Hannah, a thousand-piece puzzle of the Grand Canyon; and for my Mom, a monthly cleaning service. All wonderful gifts! We hope they are well-received.

Yet the perfect, most needed gift comes to each of us in the baby Jesus, born into our hearts on Christmas day. Knowing his gift is for *us*, not because we have been good, or because we deserve it, or because he can afford it, but because *he loves us*! As Christ told his disciples in John's Gospel, he assures us, too, of his peace. We are not to worry or fret. We continue our Advent journey with the sure hope of finding this gift of lasting peace in a tiny baby, Emmanuel, God with us!

Jesus, my gift, be my hope; be my peace!

Jennifer Christ

The Lord Journeys With Us

Go in peace! The journey you are making is under the eye of the Lord. Judges 18:6

Following a cyclical liturgical calendar means that every season comes back, again and again. Maybe this year, Advent arrived when you were eager for renewal. Maybe you took to it like a seedling, reaching for the sun, and Christmas will find you newly alive in the Lord. Maybe this year, Advent arrived when you were worn down, and this last leg of the journey to Christmas feels like entering the rocky narrows of an already treacherous path.

However we arrive at this moment, Christmas *is* coming. Its return is our cause for hope—a reminder that God is faithful to us, year after year. Now and always, he reaches out to lead us to himself. Whether we are energized or depleted, eager or haggard, the journey we are making is with the Lord.

You are the way and the truth and the life, O Lord. Order my steps and draw me closer to you!

Karla Manternach

Whatever He Wills

For you are my hope, O Lᴏʀᴅ;
>   my trust, O God, from my youth.
On you I depend from birth;
>   from my mother's womb you are my strength.

Psalm 71:5-6

When life is not going according to our own plans, a little invitation arrives in our spiritual in-box. The words of God suggest it is time to move our hope away from the future we create for ourselves and hope only in God. God's mysterious ways are beautifully beyond us and our own limited imaginings—and we can be grateful for this. This is, I imagine, how Elizabeth might have named her experience when she found herself pregnant with John the Baptist. This is the story that many of our faithful ancestors tell us: The God of hope is ready to surprise us and change things. We respond with trust in God when we cooperate, when we allow God to do with us whatever he wills. What is the story that our lives will tell our descendants? Is it a story of hope and trust?

Sr. Julia Walsh, F.S.P.A.

December 18

Even in Sadness

In all circumstances give thanks, for this is the will of God for you in Christ Jesus. 1 Thessalonians 5:18

The writer Wendell Berry once entreated his readers to "Be joyful, though you have considered all the facts." That's pretty good advice and certainly in keeping with the encouragement Paul, Silvanus and Timothy gave to the church of Thessalonica.

During this busy time of year, there are ample opportunities for giving thanks, filled as it is for many with the joys of family, friends and receiving gifts. But there are also the other "circumstances" of our lives, "all the facts" that can often make it difficult to be thankful or joyful. Christmas can be a painful time as we remember those no longer with us. But even in that sadness, God calls us to find small grains of gratitude and offer them back in thanksgiving for the gift of life and for those whom we have loved.

God, even in my pain, I thank you.

Steve Givens

A Beacon of Hope

Amen, I say to you, whatever you did for one of these least brothers of mine, you did for me. Matthew 25:40

All my ten-year-old daughter wanted for Christmas last year was money to feed the homeless. Her friend found out and had Santa deliver some snacks for the project. On the big day, we loaded up our minivan with bagged lunches, water bottles and blankets. We drove around the city of Boston and handed everything out.

My daughter did more that day than feed the bodies of the homeless. She fed their souls with hope. Someone noticed. Someone cared and took action. We watched that hope ripple out when we circled back and saw one recipient sharing his lunch with a new friend. My daughter's heart was filled to the brim.

No matter our age, God calls each of us to be a beacon of hope for those around us. When we are, we find that same hope reflected back to us in spades.

Heavenly Father, inspire me to be a beacon of hope to those in need.

Claire McGarry

Something Amazing

The Lord's acts of mercy are not exhausted,
   his compassion is not spent;
They are renewed each morning—
   great is your faithfulness! Lamentations 3:22-23

When the weather changed, I reached for a heavier coat, not worn since last winter. In the pocket I found a missing set of keys. I'd forgotten about them. Maybe because we are able to forget important things, like keys, so easily, we find it amazing that God will never forget us. Sure, we are God's beloved; we call ourselves the children of God. How do we know this? Advent reminds us that God planned something amazing for us from the beginning. We wait in hopeful anticipation, like all children before Christmas day, knowing God will never forsake us.

Eternal God, in the rising of the sun each morning, my hope in your mercy is renewed.

Deborah A. Meister

Greater Hope and Joy

**Blessed be the Lord, the God of Israel;
for he has come to his people and set them free.** Luke 1:68

We have done many good things in our life, but sometimes we have done things that need God's forgiveness. The good news is that God's love and forgiveness are always within us. No matter what we do, that will never change, for it is the very nature of God to be unceasingly forgiving. It is through his loving forgiveness that God has brought redemption to us; for our awareness of divine forgiveness has redeemed us from guilt and fear, and enabled us to love and to trust. As we prepare during Advent to celebrate Christ's birth, we can ask ourselves how our awareness of his divine redemptive love has brought us greater hope and joy. Appreciating what Christ's forgiveness has meant for us will help us to celebrate his birth with greater love and gratitude.

Lord, may our Advent reflections help us to recognize more deeply how much you love us.

Fr. Kenneth E. Grabner, C.S.C.

THE RESHAPING

> Every valley shall be lifted up,
>> every mountain and hill made low;
> The rugged land shall be a plain,
>> the rough country, a broad valley. Isaiah 40:4

Whenever I hear this passage from Isaiah, especially during the Advent season, I'm struck anew by its unwavering language. Isaiah doesn't write that the valley might be raised up or the mountains might be leveled or that uneven earth might be smoothed over, as if all these rearrangements are mere and remote possibilities. Instead, the prophet deliberately employs the word shall. Everything that is in need of reordering *shall* be changed. Not only might it happen, it is already in process.

And the reshaping of this landscape is not only geographic and external. What is rugged and rough, crooked and bent, in need of a straight path in our souls is being called to change, and conversion of heart is being invited into the deep inner soul work of genuine transformation. With God's grace, this shall happen in our lives.

God who makes all things new, I place my hope in your promise of what shall be.

Sr. Chris Koellhoffer, I.H.M.

With Faith and Hope

> **When Elizabeth heard Mary's greeting, the infant leaped in her womb, and Elizabeth, filled with the holy Spirit, cried out in a loud voice...** Luke 1:41-42

What surrounds you in these last days before Christmas? The joy of beautiful relationships and celebrations? The dread of feeling loneliness, isolation, broken or harmful relationships? The oppression of expectations, commitments and activity? The grief of death?

We carry them all, and we are asked and urged to carry them together in these final Advent days. As Advent comes to a close, we accompany Mary, Joseph and the unborn Redeemer on their journey to birth. We experience how God has come among us, not in ideas or imagination, but in the flesh, more real than the earth under our feet. We let the flame of faith and hope leap inside us. We let the Holy Spirit who dwells in us burst forth in loud song. We are overshadowed by these women of faith, Elizabeth and Mary, and their children—John, who prepared the way, and Jesus, who opened it to every one of us.

Let us sing your praises, Lord, on the harp and with our lives!

Mary Marrocco

December 24

The Best Christmas Gift

"...Emmanuel,"
which means "God is with us." Matthew 1:23

I regularly meet with people who have lost hope. Recently, I prayed with a man going through a painful divorce, also with a scrupulous young man riddled with fear and likewise with a daughter whose father was murdered. All of them were struggling with an apparently absent God.

I cannot fix any of these terrible tragedies. But I do sit with them. I listen to their anguish. And I suffer with them. Perhaps this is what God does. God sits with us, especially in the dark times, and in the person of Jesus suffers with us.

The name we give to Jesus on this blessed day is Emmanuel, God with us. Can there be any better or more important gift in our lives than God's loving presence?

Lord, I do not ask that you take all the crosses from my life. Rather, I pray that you be with me and in me so that I may faithfully endure whatever comes.

Msgr. Stephen J. Rossetti

Eyes to the Future

Living is the spirit of those who fear the Lord,
for their hope is in their savior.
Whoever fear the Lord are afraid of nothing
and are never discouraged, for he is their hope.

Sirach 34:14-16

The Christmas season can be all about memories—a child's joy over opening a special gift; the fun of decorating or baking with family or friends; the beauty of the parish crèche. Who among us hasn't pulled out old photos to relive simpler, happier times?

Looking back is good but only to a point, as Lot's wife learned. Christians keep their eyes looking forward. With Christ as our hope, we need fear no earthly situation, regardless of how oppressive it is. Because we believe, we can choose to live boldly and with confidence. Because we believe, we live with confidence. Because we believe, we live in faith and the hope of a future in heaven.

Jesus, I fear nothing, for you have become my hope.

Melanie Rigney

WAY TO LIVE

I am the way and the truth and the life. No one comes to the Father except through me. John 14:6

Good and gracious Brother Jesus, hear my prayer...

When I am at the crossroads of life, or the ruts and detours of temptation surface and I do not know the way to turn, help me go to you and recall that *you are the way*.

When harsh words and unfair judgments cloud my vision, or when I desire to keep pace with the crowd through idle gossip, help me to go to you and recall that *you are the truth*.

When darkness overcomes me and the clouds of depression and anger overtake my inner hope, and I feel as though I am dying inside, help me to go to you and recall that *you are the life*.

Teach me the way. Guide me in the truth. Bring me to life in the Spirit. Give me HOPE.

Jesus, I believe that you are the Way, the Truth and the Life.

Sr. Bridget Haase, O.S.U.

HOPE IS EVERGREEN

**Trust in the LORD with all your heart,
on your own intelligence do not rely.** Proverbs 3:5

The surgeon said he was ninety-nine percent sure the lump was benign. She was 36 years old and the mother of two. But the lump turned out to be malignant, and she needed a mastectomy. She looked for options with guarantees, but of course, none existed. She worried about her kids, and I worried about her. How do you move with the shadow of cancer in your life?

I tried to find something that might lift her spirits. It came in the form of a scrawny evergreen tree, barely a foot tall. I snuck it in her backyard and decorated it. She laughed because it was so tiny, and she cried because it looked so vulnerable and full of hope. What once was a little tree now towers over my friend's house. She is rooted in faith because gratitude long ago replaced her need for guarantees.

Shield us, Lord, when storms come our way.

Gail Goleas

DECEMBER 28

God Still Speaks

Faith is the realization of what is hoped for and evidence of things not seen. Hebrews 11:1

I imagine that each of the characters of the Nativity story felt more than surprised by how their hopes for a Messiah were fulfilled. Mary, Joseph, shepherds: many had to adjust and see that Love was incarnate right in front of them—the story of salvation was unfolding in their lives. Did they feel unworthy or confused? Did they struggle to believe? Were they overwhelmed or uncertain?

No matter who we are and what the circumstances of our life are, God is working in each of our lives. God is still speaking, and we are each a part of salvation history. If we open our hearts, what will we realize that our faith and hope is creating? What sort of evidence of God's love are we offering the world?

Sr. Julia Walsh, F.S.P.A.

FOREVER NEW CREATIONS

So whoever is in Christ is a new creation: the old things have passed away; behold, new things have come.

2 Corinthians 5:17

There's nothing like the beginning of a new year to ignite something in us for change and renewal. We make promises to eat healthier and work out. We decide it's time to mend fences and commit (yet again) to drawing closer to God in prayer and sacrament. We change our calendars and promise to change our lives.

And, indeed, all that's well and good. But what we need to remember when our fervor cools come February or March is that God is on a different schedule. God doesn't wait for the calendar, but God does wait. God waits for our approach, for our prayers and great desire for healing and renewal. Our hope is not in a new year. Our hope is in God, who is forever new and always ready to re-create us with each passing day.

In your grace, make me a new creation, God.

Steve Givens

Shining Your Light on Our World

The light shines in the darkness, and the darkness has not overcome it. John 1:5

For me, this is one of the most profoundly hopeful passages in all of Scripture. I never read it without seeing a newsreel of images playing in my mind—massacres, natural disasters, the rubble of evil acts. We are a world in darkness. How can we claim otherwise? There is so much evil, so much suffering, so much alienation and violence and loss that it can overwhelm us. This is true of our world, and it is true of our own lives. And yet no matter how bad things get (and they do get bad), goodness is never completely snuffed out, nor will it ever be. God is present in our darkest hours, a light that shines on, incorrigible, tenacious and fierce. At times it may seem like little more than a flicker. But it never goes out. One day that goodness will engulf us. We will be bathed in light forever.

God of love, I believe in you. Shine your light on all the world.

Karla Manternach

PRAYERS

MORNING PRAYERS

Christ, my Savior, in the still freshness of this morning, I turn my heart to you. I offer you everything that will happen today in the hope that you will take the few loaves and fish of my life and make another miracle. If it be your will, my hopes, my dreams and all my efforts will serve you and your people. AMEN.

The dawn of a new day brings with it fresh possibilities through your mercy, O Lord. Fill me not with regret over yesterday or worry about tomorrow, but confidence and courage to live in the freedom of the present moment. Here you abide with me in a foretaste of eternal life. Open my heart to receive the good gifts you will offer me today, sure to be enough to sustain me. I ask this through Jesus Christ, your Son and our Lord. AMEN.

Thank you, Father, for the refreshment of a good night's rest. In the dawning of another day, I take this moment to place myself in your hands and ask that you renew my faith, my hope and my love for you and all those around me. May all that I do today bring you greater praise, glory and honor. AMEN.

Lord Jesus, I awake this morning aware of people who need my prayers, and so I bring them to you in hope and trust that you will give them what they need. I especially ask that you give them a sense of your presence and love. At the same time, strengthen me to be your presence to everyone I meet today. Slow me down so that I can recognize opportunities to serve others in your name.

Amen.

Lord, give me a heart filled with gratitude as this morning unfolds. When I am inclined to see "the same old thing," remind me that each moment comes from your hand, fresh with possibility and new hope. May I never take for granted the people you put in my life, but graciously receive the blessing of their presence and humbly learn from them, according to your will. Amen.

EVENING PRAYERS

Gracious God, you have given me the gift of life so that I might have the fullness of joy through Jesus, your Son. As this day draws to a close, I place myself in your hands. May all my worries, concerns and fears dissolve in confidence that your mercy will last forever. Renew in me the hope for a brighter future, faith in your providential care and love for those nearest to me, especially those who need it most. Help me to grow in trust that I have done the best I could and that you will be with me all the days of my life.

Amen.

Lord, you search my heart, and so you know my worries and fears as well as my joys and delights. I place all these things in your hands: the good and the bad alike. Give me the trust I need to let go of the past and hope in the future, whether I can control that or not. May this night bring me a renewal in body, mind and spirit so that I can rise refreshed tomorrow to do your will. AMEN.

Lord, I place in your hands the unfinished business of the day, the hopes I had at its beginning and the regrets I have now at its end. Thank you for the times I felt your presence in the satisfaction of accomplishment and the enjoyment of your good creation, especially the people you have placed in my life. AMEN.

Thank you, Lord Jesus, for all the gifts of this day, especially those I have not noticed. Help me to see where I have fallen short of true discipleship so that I can ask forgiveness and receive your healing mercy. As this day draws to a close, give my spirit deep rest and confidence in you so that I can rise tomorrow renewed in faith, hope and love. AMEN.

Almighty and Eternal God, your forgiveness and love give me peace at the end of this day. With every breath I take, your love fills me with hope. The night enfolds me in darkness, while your Spirit illuminates my memory of all that I have experienced today. Help me to discern in these experiences what I need to learn in order to best serve your will. Amen.

FOR LENT

Lord Jesus, you know best what we need to grow in faith, hope and love. As we observe this Lent through prayer, fasting and charitable works, may we be open to whatever gifts your Holy Spirit offers us. May we live our baptismal promises with greater fidelity for our good and the good of the whole world. Amen.

FOR EASTER

God of all goodness, in a burst of resurrection light, you overthrew the powers of darkness. May our celebration of the Easter season strengthen us in hope for a brighter future than we can possibly imagine. May our faith in your power and goodness grow stronger throughout these 50 days. And may we learn to love others as you have loved us. Amen.

A PRAYER OF REMEMBRANCE

O God, our hearts are saddened by the memory of those we have lost. At the same time, we celebrate the goodness of their lives even as we hope to see them again. We remember especially those who have given their lives in military service protecting those who could not protect themselves. May their families find consolation and hope in you. May you also strengthen those who must have to face the scourges of war and the difficult challenges of peace.

Amen.

FOR ECONOMIC SECURITY

Lord, you are the rock of our lives, the source of all true stability. Grant that your people might find their security in you first of all. Help them to find meaningful employment during their working years and a measure of comfort in their retirement. Help us all to learn to live within our means so that we can help those in our neighborhoods and across the globe who have less than we do. Replace the fear in our hearts with gratitude, and give us confidence in your providence. May we hope in the future and in the blessings and opportunities of today. Amen.

FOR INNER PEACE

Lord, deliver me from my worries, fears and regrets and take away my shame. Help me to place my greatest troubles in your hands and to trust that you will bring healing to my weary soul. Amen.

FOR UNITY IN THE CHURCH

Lord Jesus, you are the cornerstone of our faith and the essential building block of our Church. Whenever we forget that simple truth, we begin to divide according to human standards and against your will. As we strive with sincere hearts to proclaim the Gospel in word and deed, send your Holy Spirit down upon us so that we might always be your faithful, hopeful and loving people.

Amen.

FOR ENCOURAGEMENT

Lord, my spirits are at a low ebb due to circumstances beyond my control. I don't want to complain and mope all the time, but I am sorely tempted to do just that. Help me to acknowledge not only the difficulties I face, but also the strengths I have, especially the strength to choose my own attitude. Give me the virtue of courage to take action where I can change things for the better. Give me also the grace of acceptance without bitterness where I am power-less to make a difference. Amen.

FOR ADVENT

Loving Creator of the Universe, we ask your help as we begin this season of joyful expectation. Give us the longing of your prophet Isaiah, that our hearts might not settle for anything less than the coming of your reign. Give us the honesty of John the Baptist, that we might know our need for repentance and forgiveness. Give us the courageous joy of Mary, that we might become true disciples in spite of moments of uncertainty and sorrow. Lastly, dear God, give us patience, that we might wait in hope for all your gifts to us.

Amen.

FOR CHRISTMAS

Word Made Flesh, you came to share our humanity so that we might share your divinity. As our voices rise in praise throughout this Christmas season, we pray that the good news of your birth might spread far and wide, to a world that is sorely in need of your love. Amen.

ACT OF HOPE

O my God, relying on your almighty power and infinite mercy and promises, I hope to obtain pardon of my sins, the help of your grace and life everlasting, through the merits of Jesus Christ, my Lord and Redeemer. Amen.

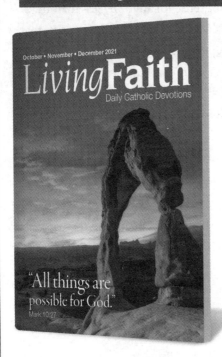